W9-CLA-948

Easy Beading

Vol. 7

Fast. Fashionable. Fun.

The best projects from the seventh year of *BeadStyle* magazine

KALMBACH BOOKS

Kalmbach Books
21027 Crossroads Circle
Waukesha, Wisconsin 53186
www.Kalmbach.com/books

Published in 2011
15 14 13 12 11   1 2 3 4 5

Printed in China

ISBN: 978-0-87116-420-9

The material in this book has appeared previously
in *BeadStyle* magazine. *BeadStyle* is registered as a
trademark.

Publisher's Cataloging-In-Publication Data

Easy beading. Vol. 7 : fast, fashionable, fun : the best
projects from the seventh year of BeadStyle magazine.

    p. : col. ill. ; cm.

    All projects have appeared previously in BeadStyle
magazine.
    ISBN: 978-0-87116-420-9

    1. Beadwork–Handbooks, manuals, etc. 2. Beads–
Handbooks, manuals, etc. 3. Jewelry making–Handbooks,
manuals, etc. I. Title: BeadStyle Magazine.

TT860 .E27 2010a
745.594/2

Contents

COVER PAGE 90

21

14 Gemstones

54

66 Crystals

16

108 Metal & chain

118

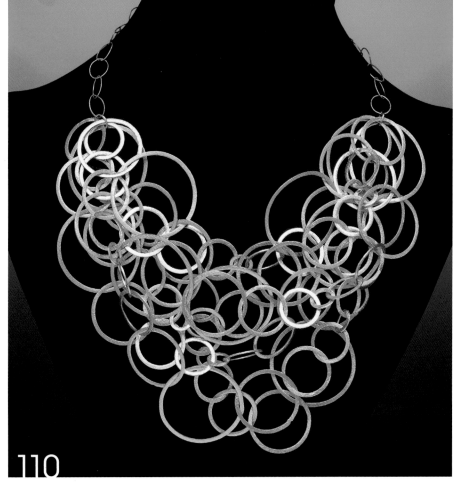

110

166

200 Mixed media

210

Introduction

Welcome to the seventh volume of *Easy Beading*. I'm happy to say there is no such thing as a "seven-year itch" in beading. We're just as smitten with beading as we were during our honeymoon year of 2003.

Each year — each project, in fact — brings us something different. There are always new materials, untried color combinations, and, of course, new designs from veteran and new beaders. Some first-time *BeadStyle* contributors are represented in this volume. Be sure to check out the projects by Sonia Kumar, Jess DiMeo, Leah Hanoud, Kelsey Lawler — just some of the newbies.

Easy Beading is once again organized by materials used:

• Gemstones
• Crystals
• Metal & chain
• Glass, ceramic, & pearls
• Mixed media

My favorite materials are Venetian beads (my "Beads capture Italian flavor" bracelet is on page 164) and crystals, but there are plenty of pieces for me to love in each category.

We've included projects for the beginner as well as the more experienced beader. There are pieces you can make in an hour or two and some you could tackle in 15 minutes. The following pages are packed with inspiration as well as instruction, so get ready to be delighted!

I hope you have as much fun with these projects as we did.

Warmest regards,

Cathy

**CATHY JAKICIC,
EDITOR, *BEADSTYLE* MAGAZINE**
editor@beadstylemag.com

Beader's Glossary
A visual reference to common beads and findings

gemstone shapes

lentil

rondelle

faceted
rondelle

round

oval

marquise

rectangle

tube

briolette

teardrop

chips

nugget

crystal and glass

Czech fire-polished

bicone

top-drilled bicone

cube

oval

drop

briolette

cone

round

saucer

top-drilled saucer
(with jump ring)

flat back

dichroic

lampworked   glass flowers   leaves   dagger

teardrop   fringe drops   seed beads   triangle   cube   bugle

pearls, shells, and miscellaneous

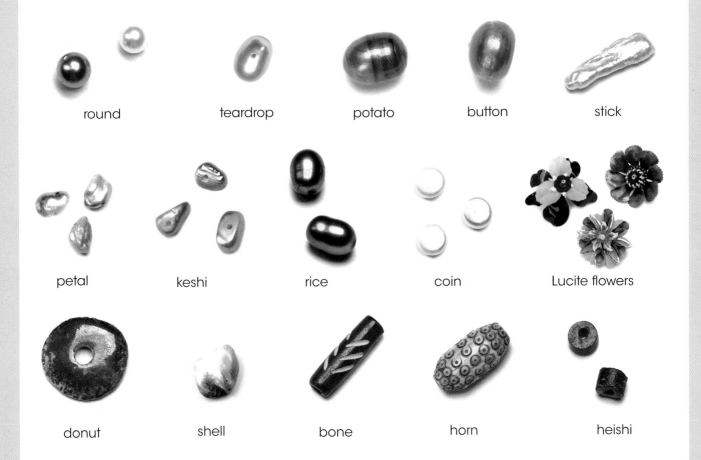

round   teardrop   potato   button   stick

petal   keshi   rice   coin   Lucite flowers

donut   shell   bone   horn   heishi

findings, spacers, and connectors

French hook ear wires   post earring   hoop earring   lever-back earring   ear thread   magnetic clasp   S-hook clasp

lobster claw clasp   toggle clasp   two-strand toggle clasp   box clasp   slide clasp   hook-and-eye clasps   snap clasp

pinch crimp end   crimp ends   coil end   crimp cone   tube bail with loop   tube-shaped and round crimp beads   crimp covers   bead tips

jump rings and soldered jump rings   split ring   spacers   bead caps   pinch bail   multistrand spacer bars

two-strand curved tube   single-strand tube   3-to-1 and 2-to-1 connectors   chandelier component   bail   cone

tools, stringing materials, and chain

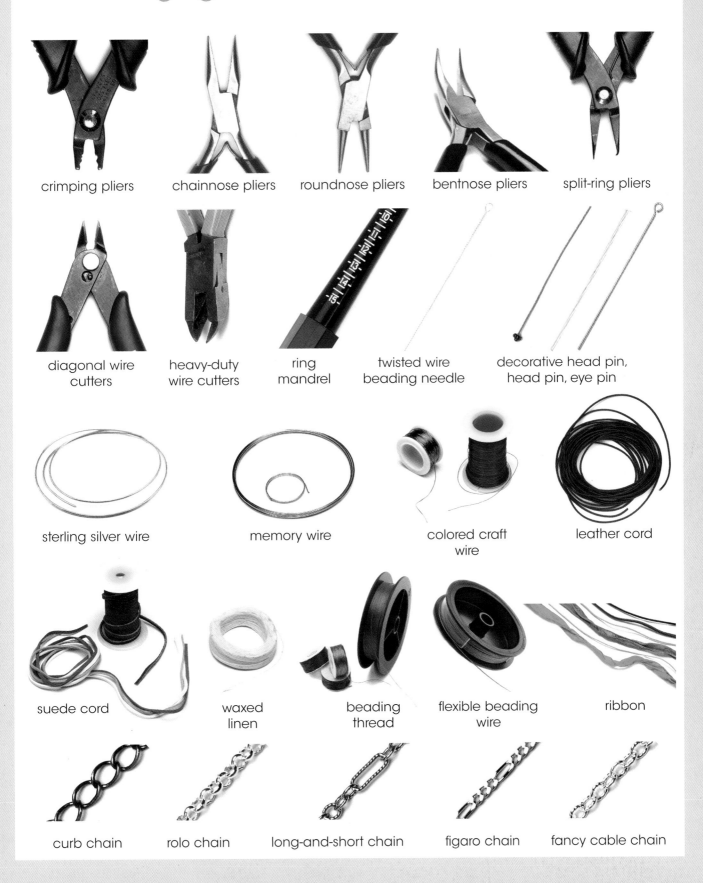

crimping pliers

chainnose pliers

roundnose pliers

bentnose pliers

split-ring pliers

diagonal wire cutters

heavy-duty wire cutters

ring mandrel

twisted wire beading needle

decorative head pin, head pin, eye pin

sterling silver wire

memory wire

colored craft wire

leather cord

suede cord

waxed linen

beading thread

flexible beading wire

ribbon

curb chain

rolo chain

long-and-short chain

figaro chain

fancy cable chain

Basics

A step-by-step reference to key jewelry-making techniques used in bead-stringing projects

plain loop

Trim the wire or head pin ⅜ in. (1 cm) above the top bead. Make a right-angle bend close to the bead.

Grab the wire's tip with round-nose pliers. The tip of the wire should be flush with the pliers. Roll the wire to form a half circle. Release the wire.

Reposition the pliers in the loop and continue rolling.

The finished loop should form a centered circle above the bead.

wrapped loop

Make sure you have at least 1¼ in. (3.2 cm) of wire above the bead. With the tip of your chainnose pliers, grasp the wire directly above the bead. Bend the wire (above the pliers) into a right angle.

Using roundnose pliers, position the jaws in the bend.

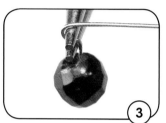

Bring the wire over the top jaw of the roundnose pliers.

Reposition the pliers' lower jaw snugly into the loop. Curve the wire downward around the roundnose pliers. This is the first half of a wrapped loop.

Position the chainnose pliers' jaws across the loop.

Wrap the wire tail around the wire stem, covering the stem between the loop and the top bead. Trim the excess wire and press the cut end close to the wraps with chainnose pliers.

opening and closing loops or jump rings

Hold the loop or jump ring with two pairs of chainnose pliers or chainnose and roundnose pliers, as shown.

To open the loop or jump ring, bring one pair of pliers toward you and push the other pair away. String materials on the open loop or jump ring. Reverse the steps to close the open loop or jump ring.

opening a split ring

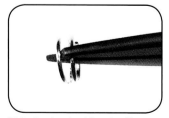

Slide the hooked tip of split-ring pliers between the two overlapping wires.

overhand knot

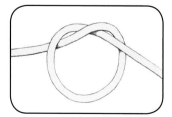

Make a loop and pass the working end through it. Pull the ends to tighten the knot.

surgeon's knot

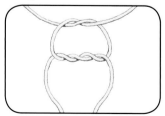

Cross the right end over the left end and go through the loop. Go through again. Pull the ends to tighten. Cross the left end over the right end and go through once. Pull the ends to tighten.

lark's head knot

Fold a cord in half and lay it behind a ring, loop, etc. with the fold pointing down. Bring the ends through the ring from back to front, then through the fold and tighten.

12

making wraps above a top-drilled bead

1

Center a top-drilled bead on a 3-in. (7.6 cm) piece of wire. Bend each wire upward to form a squared-off "U" shape.

2

Cross the wires into an "X" above the bead.

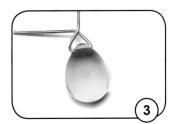

3

Using chainnose pliers, make a small bend in each wire to form a right angle.

4

Wrap the horizontal wire around the vertical wire as in a wrapped loop. Trim the excess wire.

folded crimp

1

Position the crimp bead in the notch closest to the crimping pliers' handle.

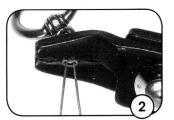

2

Separate the wires and firmly squeeze the crimp.

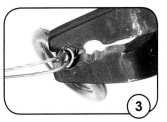

3

Move the crimp into the notch at the pliers' tip and hold the crimp as shown. Squeeze the crimp bead, folding it in half at the indentation.

4

Test that the folded crimp is secure.

flat crimp

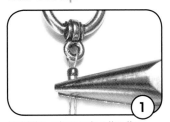

1

Hold the crimp using the tip of your chainnose pliers. Squeeze the pliers firmly to flatten the crimp.

2

Tug the wire to make sure the crimp has a solid grip. If the wire slides, repeat the steps with a new crimp.

cutting flexible beading wire

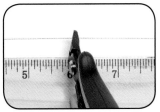

Decide how long you want your necklace to be. Add 6 in. (15 cm) and cut a piece of beading wire to that length. (For a bracelet, add 5 in./13 cm.)

add a clasp

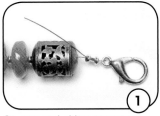

1

On one end, string a spacer, a crimp bead, a spacer, and a clasp. Go back through the last few beads strung and tighten the wire.

2

On the other end of the beaded section, repeat step 2, substituting a 3–4-in. (7.6–10 cm) piece of chain for the clasp if desired. On each end, crimp the crimp bead and trim the excess wire. Close a crimp cover over each crimp, if desired.

Gemstones

Winter GEMSTONE necklace

These beads show off both the warm and cool colors possible with amazonite.

Gunmetal chain brings out the moody hues of a seasonal set

by Stacy Werkheiser

Black gold amazonite rondelles remind me of the cool colors of a snowy winter night. The varied colors of the strand — blue, green, taupe, and grey — make it look like you spent hours selecting the beads, while gunmetal chain and spacers unify the design. I love the splash of red on the pendant; it heralds the dawn of a bright (if not quite warm) morning.

1 necklace • Decide how long you want your necklace to be and cut a piece of chain to that length. On a 3-in. (7.6 cm) head pin, string a coin bead. Make the first half of a wrapped loop (Basics, p. 12). Attach the center link of chain and complete the wraps.

2 On a 1½-in. (3.8 cm) head pin, string a spacer and a rondelle. Make the first half of a wrapped loop. Make six rondelle units.

Supplies

necklace 19 in. (48 cm)
- 28–32 mm gemstone coin bead
- 16-in. (41 cm) strand 5–6 mm gemstone rondelles
- **30–36** 3 mm round spacers
- flexible beading wire, .014 or .015
- 18–20 in. (46–51 cm) chain, 10–12 mm links
- 3-in. (7.6 cm) decorative head pin
- **6** 1½-in. (3.8 cm) head pins
- **2** 5–6 mm jump rings
- **2** crimp beads
- two-strand toggle clasp
- chainnose and roundnose pliers
- diagonal wire cutters
- crimping pliers (optional)

earrings
- **4** 5–6 mm gemstone rondelles left over from necklace
- **4** 3 mm round spacers
- **2** 1½-in. (3.8 cm) head pins
- pair of earring wires
- chainnose and roundnose pliers
- diagonal wire cutters

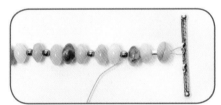

3 On each side of the pendant, attach three rondelle units, skipping a few links in between. Complete the wraps as you go.

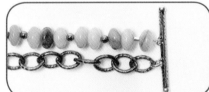

4 Cut a piece of beading wire (Basics). Center a spacer, two rondelles, and a spacer. On each side, string: three rondelles, spacer, rondelle, spacer, three rondelles, spacer, two rondelles, spacer. Repeat until the strand is 3 in. (7.6 cm) shorter than the chain.

5 On each end, string two rondelles and attach half of a two-strand toggle clasp (Basics).

6 On each end, open a jump ring (Basics) and attach the chain and the remaining loop of the clasp. Close the jump ring.

1 earrings • On a head pin, string a spacer, two rondelles, and a spacer. Make a wrapped loop (Basics).

2 Open the loop of an earring wire (Basics) and attach the dangle. Close the loop. Make a second earring.

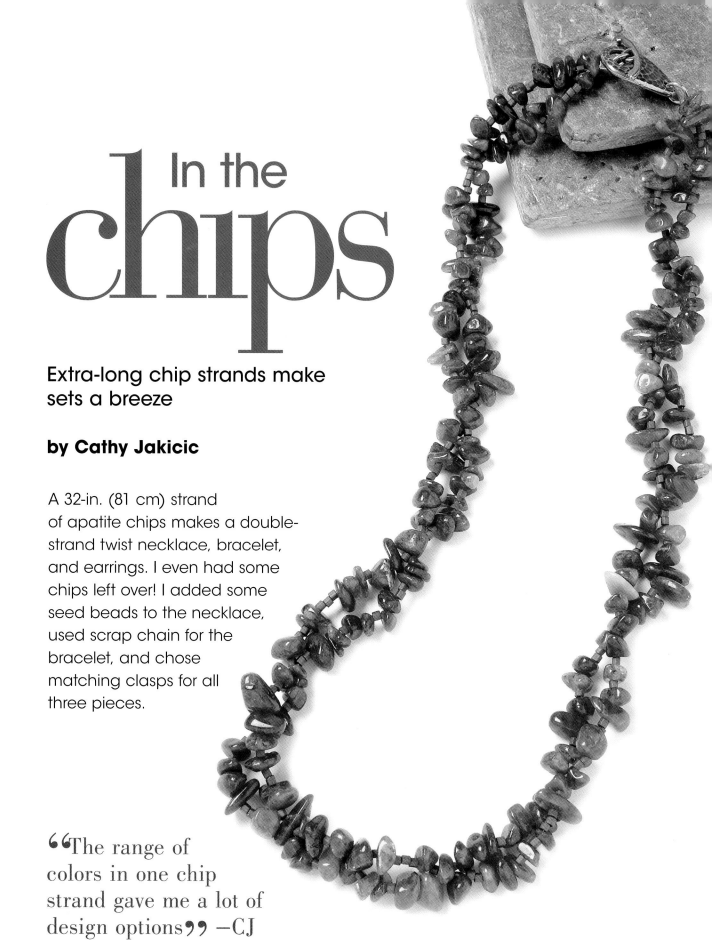

In the chips

Extra-long chip strands make sets a breeze

by Cathy Jakicic

A 32-in. (81 cm) strand of apatite chips makes a double-strand twist necklace, bracelet, and earrings. I even had some chips left over! I added some seed beads to the necklace, used scrap chain for the bracelet, and chose matching clasps for all three pieces.

66The range of colors in one chip strand gave me a lot of design options**99** —CJ

1 necklace • Cut two 25-in. (64 cm) pieces of beading wire. Center a chip over both wires (Basics, p. 12).

2 On each end of each wire, string 1½ in. (3.8 cm) of chips and 11º seed beads.

3 **a** On each end, string a chip over both wires.

b Repeat steps 2 and 3a until the strand is within 1 in. (2.5 cm) of the finished length. Check the fit, and add or remove beads if necessary.

4 Open a jump ring (Basics, p. 12) and attach half of a clasp. Close the jump ring. Repeat with the other half of the clasp. On each end of the strand, attach half of the clasp (Basics).

1 bracelet • On a head pin, string an 11º seed bead and three chips. Make the first half of a wrapped loop (Basics). Make 11 to 13 bead units.

2 Cut a 6–7-in. (15–18 cm) piece of chain. Attach a bead unit to the center link. Complete the wraps. Continue attaching bead units to the chain, leaving three open links between units.

Supplies

necklace 20 in. (51 cm)
- 32-in. (81 cm) strand 8–12 mm gemstone chips
- 1 g 11º seed beads
- flexible beading wire, .014 or .015
- **2** 7 mm jump rings
- **2** crimp beads
- toggle clasp
- chainnose and roundnose pliers, or **2** pairs of chainnose pliers
- diagonal wire cutters
- crimping pliers (optional)

bracelet
- **33–39** 8–12 mm gemstone chips left over from necklace
- **11–13** 11º seed beads
- 6–7 in. (15–18 cm) chain, 5 mm links
- **11–13** 2-in. (5 cm) head pins
- **2** 7 mm jump rings
- toggle clasp
- chainnose and roundnose pliers
- diagonal wire cutters

earrings
- **6** 8–12 mm gemstone chips left over from necklace
- **2** 11º seed beads
- **2** 1½-in. (3.8 cm) head pins
- **2** 7 mm jump rings
- **2** loop halves of toggle clasps
- pair of earring wires
- chainnose and roundnose pliers
- diagonal wire cutters

3 On each end, open a jump ring (Basics) and attach half of a clasp and an end link of chain. Close the jump ring.

Tip

When making the bead units in the bracelet and earrings, don't wrap the loops too tightly against the chips. Chips break more easily than other gemstone shapes.

1 earrings • Following bracelet step 1, make a bead unit using the largest part of your roundnose pliers. Attach the unit to a clasp half and complete the wraps.

2 Open a jump ring (Basics) and attach the dangle and an earring wire. Close the jump ring. Make a second earring.

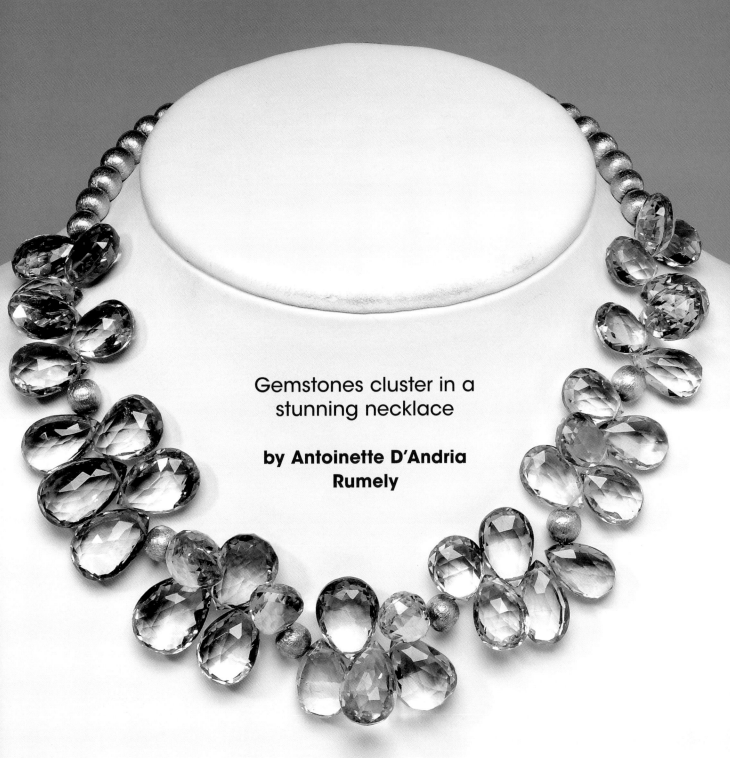

Gemstones cluster in a
stunning necklace

**by Antoinette D'Andria
Rumely**

BUNCHES
of briolettes

I'm obsessed with gemstones of all different shapes and hues, but I'm partial to pinks, purples, and greens (especially celadon). These amethyst briolettes dazzled me with their beauty, color, and clarity. The stones are miracles from the earth! For an inexpensive version, use gemstone look-alikes made from glass. The ones I used have the look of real turquoise.

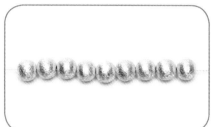

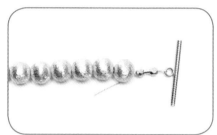

1 necklace • Cut a piece of beading wire (Basics, p. 12). String five briolettes and a metal bead. Repeat four or five times, then string five briolettes. Center the beads.

2 On each end, string metal beads until the strand is within 1 in. (2.5 cm) of the finished length.

3 On each end, attach half of a toggle clasp (Basics).

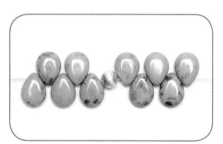

1 bracelet • Cut a piece of beading wire (Basics). String five briolettes, a metal bead, and five briolettes. Center the beads.

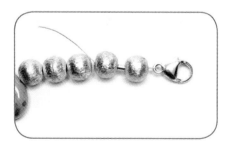

2 On each end, string metal beads until the strand is within 1 in. (2.5 cm) of the finished length. On one end, attach a lobster claw clasp (Basics). On the other end, attach a 1¼-in. (3.2 cm) piece of chain for the extender.

3 Cut a 3-in. (7.6 cm) piece of 24-gauge wire. String a briolette and make a set of wraps above it (Basics). Make the first half of a wrapped loop (Basics). Attach the end link of chain and complete the wraps.

"I've loved jewelry since childhood, as my mother had a beautiful collection of handmade original designs from Milan." —ADR

Supplies

necklace 16½ in. (41.9 cm)

- **30-35** 15–20 mm briolettes or top-drilled teardrops
- **23-30** 6–8 mm round metal beads
- **4** 3–4 mm spacers
- flexible beading wire, .014 or .015
- **2** crimp beads
- toggle clasp
- chainnose or crimping pliers
- diagonal wire cutters

bracelet

- **11** 15–20 mm briolettes or top-drilled teardrops
- **11-15** 6–8 mm round metal beads
- flexible beading wire, .014 or .015
- **3** in. (7.6 cm) 24-gauge half-hard wire
- **2** crimp beads
- lobster claw clasp
- 1¼ in. (3.2 cm) chain for extender, 5–6 mm links
- chainnose and roundnose pliers
- diagonal wire cutters
- crimping pliers (optional)

earrings

- **6** 15–20 mm briolettes or top-drilled teardrops
- **2** 6–8 mm round metal beads
- **2** 2-in. (5 cm) head pins
- pair of earring wires
- chainnose and roundnose pliers
- diagonal wire cutters

Design alternative

If you prefer more delicate jewelry, make a necklace or bracelet using small (5–6 mm) briolettes. For a variation on the earrings, make longer dangles by stringing several briolettes on each head pin.

1 earrings • On a head pin, string three briolettes and a metal bead. Make a wrapped loop (Basics).

2 Open the loop of an earring wire (Basics). Attach the dangle and close the loop. Make a second earring the mirror image of the first.

Tip

If you're buying briolettes online, take note of how many beads are on each strand. Better quality briolettes are often sold on shorter (8 in./20 cm) strands with plastic or metal spacers in between.

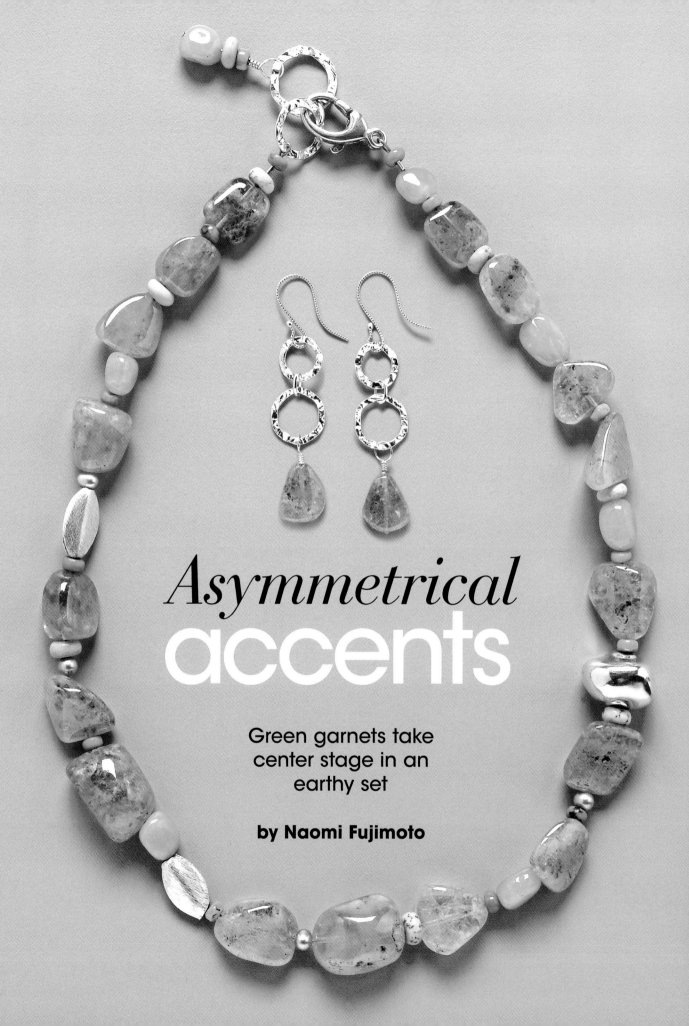

Asymmetrical accents

Green garnets take center stage in an earthy set

by Naomi Fujimoto

Take a strand of unexpectedly green garnets and use tiny rondelles as spacers to bring out their beauty. The turquoise beads, 3 mm pearls, and chrysoprase accents also extend the strand, leaving enough for a bracelet and earrings. It's up to you how many metal accent beads to include — just place them asymmetrically to play up the organic shape and style of the nuggets.

1 necklace • Cut a piece of beading wire (Basics, p. 12). Center a nugget on the wire.

2 On one end, string beads, including a metal accent bead, until the strand is half the desired length.

3 On the other end, string a different arrangement of beads, including two metal accent beads, until the strand is within 1 in. (2.5 cm) of the desired length.

4 Check the fit, and add or remove beads if necessary. On one end, attach a lobster claw clasp (Basics).

5 On the other end, attach 1 in. (2.5 cm) of chain. On a head pin, string two or three beads and make the first half of a wrapped loop (Basics). Attach the end link of chain and complete the wraps.

bracelet • Cut a piece of beading wire (Basics). String beads until the strand is within 1 in. (2.5 cm) of the finished length. Follow steps 4 and 5 of the necklace to finish.

"I used beads from my stash in shades of green and blue to brighten up the earthy nuggets." –NF

1 earrings • On a head pin, string a nugget. Make the first half of a wrapped loop (Basics).

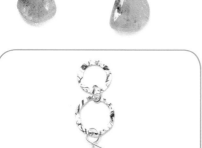

2 Cut a 1-in. (2.5 cm) piece of chain. Attach the bead unit to a link and complete the wraps.

3 Open the loop of an earring wire (Basics) and attach the dangle. Close the loop. Make a second earring.

Tip

Different strands of the same gemstone often show a variety of colors. I bought two strands of green garnet nuggets but used different accent colors to change the mood of each necklace.

Supplies

necklace 16½ in. (41.9 cm)
- 16-in. (41 cm) strand 10–25 mm nuggets
- **3** 10–15 mm metal accent beads
- **7–10** 8–12 mm gemstone beads
- **15–30** 3–6 mm rondelles, in **2** colors
- **4–8** 3–4 mm pearls
- flexible beading wire, .014 or .015
- 1½-in. (3.8 cm) head pin
- **2** crimp beads
- lobster claw clasp
- 1–2 in. (2.5–5 cm) chain for extender, 10–13 mm links
- chainnose and roundnose pliers
- diagonal wire cutters
- crimping pliers (optional)

bracelet
- **5–7** 10–25 mm nuggets left over from necklace
- **2–3** 10–15 mm metal accent beads
- **2–4** 8–12 mm gemstone beads
- **8–12** 3–6 mm rondelles, in two colors
- **2–5** 3–4 mm pearls
- flexible beading wire, .014 or .015
- 1½-in. (3.8 cm) head pin
- **2** crimp beads
- lobster claw clasp
- 1–2 in. (2.5–5 cm) chain for extender, 10–13 mm links
- chainnose and roundnose pliers
- diagonal wire cutters
- crimping pliers (optional)

earrings
- **2** 10–25 mm nuggets left over from necklace
- **3** in. (7.6 cm) chain, 10–13 mm links
- **2** 1½-in. (3.8 cm) head pins
- pair of earring wires
- chainnose and roundnose pliers
- diagonal wire cutters

To carry the seasonal theme, include flower-shaped spacers and clasps.

Breeze through a spring set

Coordinate pastel tones for a quick necklace, bracelet, and earrings ◆ by Kate Purdy

Czech glass leaves, sky-blue Peruvian opals, an oversized flower clasp — all of these elements come together in an easy jewelry set. As simple to make as they are to wear, these pieces will put you in a cheerful mood.

1 necklace • Cut a piece of beading wire (Basics, p. 12). String: 4 mm flat spacer, 5 mm flat spacer, 40 mm bead, 5 mm spacer, 4 mm spacer. Center the beads.

2 On each end, string: three 12 mm leaves, 4 mm spacer, three 12 mm leaves, 4 mm spacer, metal flower, 4 mm spacer, 3 mm spacer.

3 On each end, string 6 mm round beads until the strand is within 2 in. (5 cm) of the finished length.

4 On each end, string: 3 mm spacer, 4 mm spacer, metal leaf, crimp bead, Wire Guardian. Attach half of a toggle clasp (Basics).

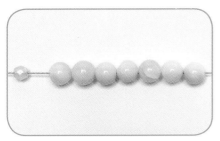

1 bracelet • Cut a piece of beading wire (Basics). String a fire-polished bead. String 6 mm round beads until the strand is within 2 in. (5 cm) of the finished length.

2 On one end, string: fire-polished bead, 3 mm spacer, metal leaf, crimp bead, Wire Guardian, bar half of a toggle clasp. Go back through the beads just strung and tighten the wire.

3 On the other end, string: 3 mm spacer, metal flower, 12 mm leaf, crimp bead, Wire Guardian. Attach the loop half of the clasp (Basics). Crimp the crimp bead on the other end and trim the excess wire.

Tip

To add length to the bracelet, string a few extra leaf beads on one end.

1 earrings • On a head pin, string a 14 mm bead, a 5 mm flat spacer, and a metal flower. Make a plain loop (Basics).

2 Open the loop of an earring wire (Basics) and attach the dangle. Close the loop. Make a second earring.

Design alternative

If you prefer warmer tones, surround a mother-of-pearl pendant with shades of peach, pink, and burgundy.

"I like Caribbean colors and tropical themes." –KP

Quick drop
bracelet

Use top-drilled beads for a top-speed set ◆ **by Joan Bailey**

Last summer, while visiting my daughter, I bought these dyed red howlite beads at a flea market. Generally, my biggest beading challenge is finding the exit at the flea market or bead store. I could spend hours there!

Supplies

bracelet
- ◆ **16-24** 14–18 mm briolettes or top-drilled beads
- ◆ **3** 5–8 mm beads
- ◆ flexible beading wire, .014 or .015
- ◆ 2-in. (5 cm) head pin
- ◆ **2** 5 mm jump rings
- ◆ **2** crimp beads
- ◆ **2** crimp covers
- ◆ toggle clasp
- ◆ chainnose and roundnose pliers
- ◆ diagonal wire cutters
- ◆ crimping pliers (optional)

earrings
- ◆ **2** 14–18 mm briolettes or top-drilled beads
- ◆ 20 in. (51 cm) 22-gauge wire
- ◆ pair of 43 mm earring wires
- ◆ chainnose and roundnose pliers
- ◆ diagonal wire cutters

1 bracelet • Cut a piece of beading wire (Basics, p. 12). String top-drilled beads until the strand is within 1 in. (2.5 cm) of the finished length.

2 Open a jump ring (Basics) and attach the bar half of a toggle clasp. Close the jump ring.
On each end, string a crimp bead and attach half of the clasp (Basics).

3 On a head pin, string three beads and make a wrapped loop (Basics).

4 Use a jump ring to attach the dangle and the bar half of the clasp.

5 Close a crimp cover over each crimp.

1 earrings • Cut a 10-in. (25 cm) piece of wire. String a top-drilled bead and make a set of wraps above it (Basics).

2 Make the first half of a wrapped loop (Basics) above the wraps. Attach the loop of an earring wire and complete the wraps. Do not trim the excess wire.

3 Use your fingers to continue wrapping the wire around the top of the bead. Trim the excess wire.

Tip

If you don't have quite enough top-drilled beads to make a bracelet, substitute a large link of chain and a lobster claw clasp to make up the difference in length.

String on the
sunny side

Master the multistrand with a striking-yet-simple necklace

by Cathy Jakicic

The combination of pink and orange is charming and unexpected. For this multitextured multistrand necklace, I added some olive green nuggets to temper the sweetness with a bit of sophistication.

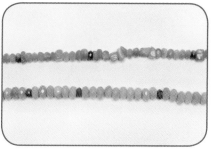

1 necklace • Cut a piece of beading wire (Basics, p. 12). Cut four more pieces, each 2 in. (5 cm) longer than the last. Set aside 15 to 20 calcite nuggets from the slab strand. On the shortest wire, string the remaining nuggets and orange calcite rondelles, interspersing fuchsia rondelles, until the strand is within 2 in. (5 cm) of the finished length. On the second wire, string rose quartz rondelles, interspersing fuchsia rondelles, until the strand is within 2 in. (5 cm) of the finished length.

2 On the third wire, string orange calcite barrels, interspersing orange calcite nuggets and fuchsia rondelles, until the strand is within 2 in. (5 cm) of the finished length. On the fourth wire, string jade nuggets, interspersing fuchsia rondelles, until the strand is within 2 in. (5 cm) of the finished length.

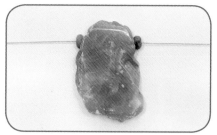

3 On the longest wire, center a fuchsia rondelle, a calcite slab, and a fuchsia rondelle.

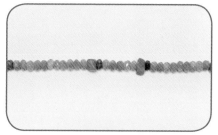

4 On each end, string orange calcite rondelles, interspersing orange calcite nuggets and fuchsia rondelles, until the strand is within 2 in. (5 cm) of the finished length.

5 Check the fit, and add or remove beads if necessary (Tip, p. 34). On each end of each strand, string: 10 11º seed beads, crimp bead, two 11ºs, Wire Guardian, the corresponding loop of half of a clasp. Go back through the beads just strung and tighten the wire. Crimp the crimp bead (Basics) and trim the excess wire.

For smaller earrings, just skip the hoop.

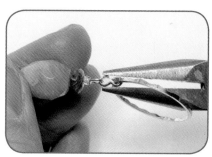

1 earrings • On a head pin, string: 11º seed bead, rondelle, barrel, rondelle, 11º. Make a plain loop (Basics).

2 Attach a connector to the bead unit and a link. Use chainnose pliers to close the loops of the connector.

3 Open the loop of an earring wire (Basics). Attach the dangle and close the loop. Make a second earring to match the first.

Design alternatives

Replace the orange calcite barrels with yellow ceramic barrels for a brighter look.

Use jade rondelles instead of nuggets to lessen the darker color's influence.

Accentuate the fuchsia by replacing the rose quartz with an entire strand of crazy lace agate.

Tip

The key to a multistrand necklace is how the strands hang together. When using different beads for each strand, simply making each strand one or two inches longer than the last won't ensure a desirable drape. Achieving the perfect look takes some extra work, but it's worth it in the end. For this necklace, I wanted the seed bead segments to be equal in length, so I made adjustments before I strung them. I attached each strand to the clasp, securing the wires with tape. Remembering that the seed beads would add 2 in. (5 cm) to each strand, I put the necklace on, evaluated how the strands looked together, and added or removed beads as needed. I did this three times before I found a drape I liked.

Supplies

necklace 16³/₄–20 in. (42.5–51 cm)

- 16-in. (41 cm) strand orange calcite slabs and nuggets*
- 16-in. (41 cm) strand 15 mm British Columbia jade nuggets
- 16-in. (41 cm) strand 12 mm orange calcite faceted barrel-shaped beads
- 16-in. (41 cm) strand 8 mm rose quartz faceted rondelles
- 2 8-in. (20 cm) strands 6 mm orange calcite faceted rondelles
- 8-in. (20 cm) strand 6 mm faceted fuchsia crazy lace agate rondelles
- 1 g 11º seed beads
- flexible beading wire, .014 or .015
- **10** crimp beads
- **10** Wire Guardians
- five-strand slide clasp
- chainnose or crimping pliers
- diagonal wire cutters

earrings

- **2** 12 mm orange calcite faceted barrel-shaped beads
- **4** 6 mm faceted fuchsia crazy lace agate rondelles
- **4** 11º seed beads
- **2** 20 mm round diamond-cut Quick Links (Beadalon, beadalon.com for retailers)
- **2** medium connectors (Beadalon)
- **2** 2-in. (5 cm) head pins
- pair of earring wires
- chainnose and roundnose pliers
- diagonal wire cutters

*Strand includes 8–10 in. (20–25 cm) of chips, four 35 mm slabs, two 55 mm slabs, and one 80 mm slab.

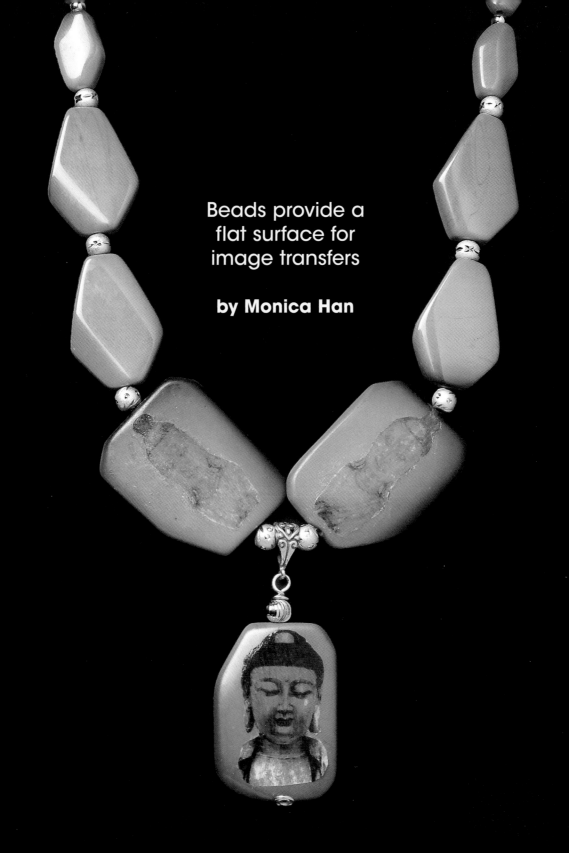

Beads provide a
flat surface for
image transfers

by Monica Han

Make a statement
of peace

Although I am not a Buddhist, I'm intrigued by the serene and peaceful influence of Buddhist sculptures and images. I often find myself admiring them when I visit museums and temples in Asia. These flat orange beads provide a smooth, bright surface for transferring images using a transfer medium.

1 picture beads • Brush Omni-Gel in a horizontal direction over the image. Allow to dry. Brush a second coat vertically. Apply a final coat diagonally. Allow to dry after each coat.

2 Cut around the image, leaving a ¼-in. (6 mm) border. Soak the image in water for 10 to 20 minutes.

3 Place the image face down on a flat 40 mm bead. With your fingers, rub away the excess paper. When you have removed most of the paper, use a lint-free towel to clean off the rest.

4 Use Omni-Gel to glue the transferred image to the bead. Make three picture beads.

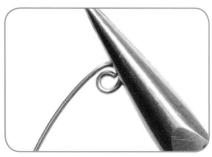

1 necklace • Cut a 4-in. (10 cm) piece of 22-gauge wire. Use the tip of your roundnose pliers to make a loop. Use chainnose pliers to turn the wire to form a coil. Bend the coil perpendicular to the stem.

2 String a 40 mm picture bead and a 6 mm bead. Make the first half of a wrapped loop (Basics, p. 12).

Supplies

picture beads
- **3** 40 mm flat beads
- **3** 28–38 mm transfer images
- container for water
- foam paintbrush
- lint-free towel
- Omni-Gel transfer medium
- scissors

necklace 18 in. (46 cm)
- **3** 40 mm flat picture beads
- **4** 32 mm flat beads
- **6–10** 20 mm flat beads
- **11** 6 mm gold beads
- **8–12** 4 mm gold spacers
- bail
- flexible beading wire, .014 or .015
- 8 in. (20 cm) 22-gauge half-hard wire
- **2** crimp beads
- toggle clasp
- chainnose and roundnose pliers
- diagonal wire cutters
- crimping pliers (optional)
- dowel, 4 mm diameter

earrings
- **2** 30 mm flat picture beads
- **2** 6 mm gold beads
- 6 in. (15 cm) 24-gauge half-hard wire
- pair of earring wires
- chainnose and roundnose pliers
- diagonal wire cutters

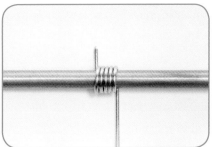

3 Attach the loop of a bail and complete the wraps. Cut one or two pieces of beading wire (Basics). Center the bail on the wires.

4 Cut a 4-in. (10 cm) piece of 22-gauge wire. Wrap one end around a dowel five times to make a wire tube. Trim the straight ends of the coil.

5 On one end of the beading wire, string the wire tube, a 6 mm bead, a picture bead, and a 6 mm bead. Repeat on the other end, omitting the wire tube (the tube will be covered by the bail).

6 On each end, string: 32 mm bead, 6 mm bead, 32 mm bead, 6 mm bead, 20 mm bead, 4 mm spacer.

7 On each end, string alternating 20 mm beads and 4 mm spacers until the strand is within 1 in. (2.5 cm) of the finished length. Attach half of a toggle clasp (Basics).

1 earrings • Make a 30 mm picture bead. Use a 3-in. (7.6 cm) piece of 24-gauge wire to make a bead unit as in necklace steps 1 and 2. Complete the wraps.

2 Open the loop of an earring wire (Basics). Attach the dangle and close the loop. Make a second earring.

Tip

Experiment with one bead first. If it doesn't work out, you can remove the image using a cotton swab and nail polish remover. Keep in mind that nail polish remover may damage the finish on some dyed beads. Test the colorfastness first on the back of the bead.

"I used gold in my design because gold is usually associated with Buddha." –MH

Pastel
preference

Build a necklace
around the muted tones
of small seashells

by Catherine Owsianiecki

I'm drawn to anything beach related and am passionate about pink. So naturally these curvy little seashell beads called to me. Highlight their subtle pinks and greens with rose quartz and jade beads. You can also wire up a pair of easy earrings.

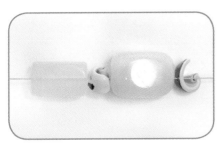

1 necklace • Cut a piece of beading wire (Basics, p. 12). String a rectangle bead, a shell bead, a nugget, and a shell. Repeat until the strand is within 2 in. (5 cm) of the finished length.

2 Cut a second piece of beading wire 2 in. (5 cm) longer than the first. String a nugget, a shell, a rectangle, and a shell. Repeat until the strand is within 2 in. (5 cm) of the finished length.

3 On each end of each wire, string a spacer, a crimp bead, and a spacer. On each side, over both wires, string a dragonfly connector. Go back through the last few beads strung and tighten the wires. Crimp the crimp beads (Basics) and trim the excess wire. Attach an S-hook to one side.

Tip

To make a set of wraps for the earrings, hold the loop with pliers and use your fingers to loosely wrap and overlap the wire.

Supplies

necklace 20 in. (51 cm)
- **2** 12-in. (30 cm) strands 20 mm nuggets
- **2** 12-in. (30 cm) strands 17 mm rectangle beads
- **2** 7-in. (18 cm) strands 10 mm shell beads
- **8** 3 mm spacers
- flexible beading wire, .018 or .019
- **4** crimp beads
- **2** dragonfly connectors
- S-hook clasp

- chainnose or crimping pliers
- diagonal wire cutters

earrings
- **2** 17 mm rectangle beads
- **4** 10 mm shell beads
- **32** in. (81 cm) 20-gauge half-hard wire
- pair of earring wires
- chainnose and roundnose pliers
- diagonal wire cutters

66My favorite material to work with is anything that's evocative of the sea — and if it's pink, all the better!99 —CO

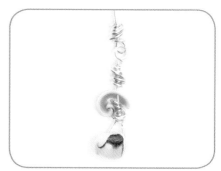

1 earrings • Cut an 8-in. (20 cm) piece of wire. About 3 in. (7.6 cm) from one end, string a shell bead and make a loose set of wraps above it (Basics).

2 String a shell and make a wrapped loop with loose wraps.

3 Cut an 8-in. (20 cm) piece of wire. About 3 in. (7.6 cm) from one end, make the first half of a wrapped loop. Attach the shell dangle and make a loose set of wraps.

4 String a rectangle bead and make a wrapped loop with loose wraps.

5 Open the loop of an earring wire (Basics). Attach the dangle and close the loop. Make a second earring.

Design alternative

If you want to include pink nuggets in your earrings, here are two other options.

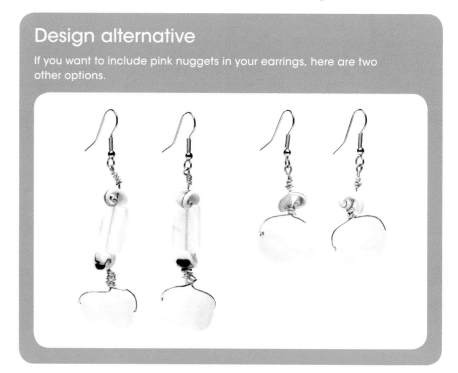

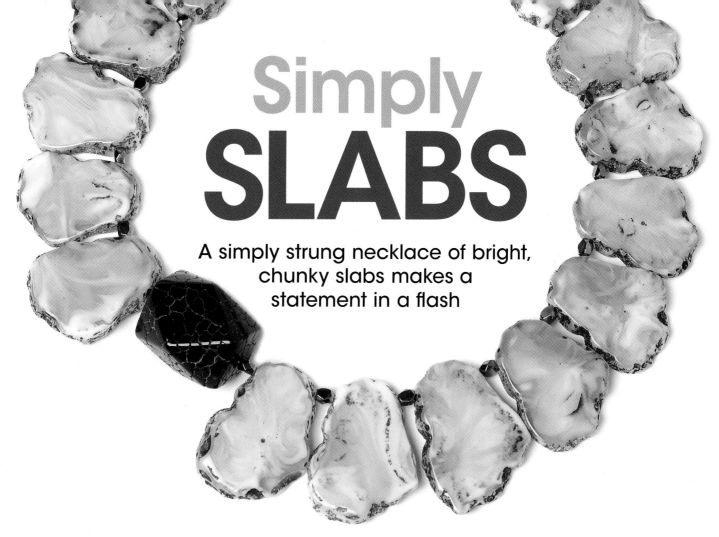

Simply SLABS

A simply strung necklace of bright, chunky slabs makes a statement in a flash

by Kelsey Lawler

A necklace doesn't have to be eight strands, choked with chain, and wrapped in wire to turn heads. Let the beads do the work!

1 Cut a piece of beading wire (Basics, p. 12). String an accent bead.

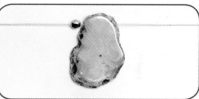

2 On each end, string a 4 mm bead and a slab. Repeat, stringing more beads on one end than the other, until the strand is within 1 in. (2.5 cm) of the finished length.

Supplies

necklace 14–16 in. (36–41 cm)
- 16-in. (41 cm) strand 30–35 mm stone slabs, top drilled
- 24–30 mm accent bead
- **20–24** 4 mm beads
- flexible beading wire, .014 or .015
- **2** crimp beads
- lobster claw clasp and soldered jump ring
- chainnose or crimping pliers
- diagonal wire cutters

3 On one end, attach a lobster claw clasp (Basics). On the other end, attach a soldered jump ring.

Tip

Slabs come in all shapes and shades — streamline your search by visiting thefind.com and searching "slab beads."

A gemstone nugget balances this fancy clasp.

1 Get some closure

Clothing clasps move up in the world — to your neckline!

by Paulette Biedenbender

If you scour enough bead stores, shows, and catalogs, you start to see the same jewelry clasps over and over again. So imagine my joy when I found a cache of clothing clasps at the fabric store! Made of base metal, these clasps are an economical option. And because the clasps are designed to add decorative detail to clothing, they pack a style punch. I placed my gunmetal clasp off to the side of my necklace, then added Chinese turquoise, onyx, and African picture jasper to complement the dark finish.

1 necklace • Cut two pieces of beading wire (Basics, p. 12). Over both wires, center a nugget. On one end, over both wires, string a repeating pattern of an 11º seed bead and an 8 mm round bead for 8–8½ in. (20–21.6 cm). End with an 11º.

3 On the second wire, string: 3 mm, 11º, 8 mm, 11º, 3 mm, 11º, coin, 11º. Repeat the pattern for 7½–8 in. (19.1–20 cm). String a 3 mm, an 11º, a 3 mm, and an 11º.

5 On the other end, over both wires, string a crimp bead and a coin. Attach the other half of the clasp.

2 On the other end, on one wire, string an 11º and a 3 mm round bead. String: 11º, coin bead, 11º, 8 mm, 11º, 3 mm, 11º, 8 mm. Repeat the pattern for 8½–9 in. (21.6–23 cm). String an 11º, a 3 mm, and an 11º.

4 On the same end, over both wires, string: 3 mm, 11º, 8 mm, 11º, crimp bead, coin. Attach half of a hook-and-eye clothing clasp (Basics).

1 bracelet • Cut two pieces of beading wire (Basics). On one wire, string: 11º seed bead, 3 mm round bead, 11º, coin bead, 11º, 3 mm, 11º, 8 mm round bead. Repeat the pattern until the strand is within 2 in. (5 cm) of the finished length, ending with an 11º, a 3 mm, and an 11º.

2 On the other wire, string: 11º, 3 mm, 11º, 8 mm, 11º, coin, 11º, 8 mm. Repeat the pattern until the strand is within 2 in. (5 cm) of the finished length, ending with an 11º, a 3 mm, and an 11º.

3 On each end, over both wires, string an 8 mm, a crimp bead, and a 3 mm. Attach half of a toggle clasp (Basics).

1 earrings • On a head pin, string an 8 mm round bead, an 11º seed bead, and an 8 mm. Make a plain loop (Basics).

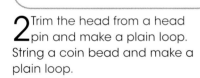

2 Trim the head from a head pin and make a plain loop. String a coin bead and make a plain loop.

3 Open the loop (Basics) of the round-bead unit and attach one loop of the coin-bead unit. Close the loop. Open the loop of the dangle and attach an earring post. Close the loop. Make a second earring.

Design alternative

This project got me wondering what other clothing clasps have been hiding at the fabric store. Here are a few one- and two-hole varieties I found.

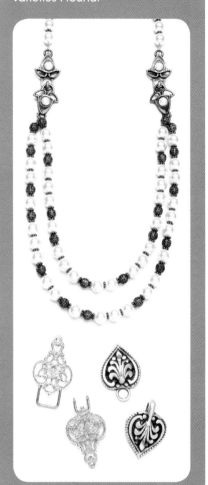

Turquoise
times two

Turquoise and silver unite in a quick set

by Jane Konkel

Like many beaders, I'm drawn to turquoise. And I'm not some fair-weather fan. I like the radiant, sky-blue variety — like these nuggets from the copper-rich Compitos mine in Mexico. I also love these earthy green chips. Traditional Hill Tribes silver complements the shiny inclusions in the nuggets.

1 necklace • Cut a piece of beading wire (Basics, p. 12). String a spacer, a chip, a spacer, and a nugget. Repeat twice. String a spacer, a chip, and a spacer. Center the beads.

2 On each end, string an accent bead, a spacer, a nugget, and a spacer. Repeat, then string an accent bead. String the pattern in step 1 until the strand is within 1 in. (2.5 cm) of the finished length.

3 On each end, attach half of a toggle clasp (Basics). To make a hook clasp instead, see p. 47.

1 bracelet • Cut a piece of beading wire (Basics). Center: spacer, chip, spacer, nugget, spacer, chip, spacer.

2 On each end, string an accent bead. String a spacer, a chip, a spacer, and a nugget, repeating until the strand is within 1 in. (2.5 cm) of the finished length.

3 On one end, attach a lobster claw clasp (Basics). Repeat on the other end, substituting a soldered ring for the clasp.

1 earrings • On a head pin, string a seed bead, a spacer, an accent bead, and a spacer. Make the first half of a wrapped loop (Basics).

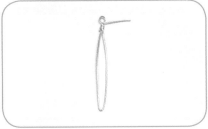

2 Follow steps 1 and 2 of the hook clasp (p. 47), making a wrapped loop with the straight wire.

3 Attach the bead unit and complete the wraps. Shape the wire into an elongated diamond.

4 Open the loop of an earring wire (Basics) and attach the dangle. Close the loop. Make a second earring.

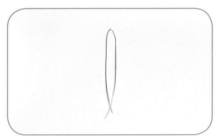

1 hook clasp • Cut an 8-in. (20 cm) piece of 18-gauge wire. Fold the wire in half.

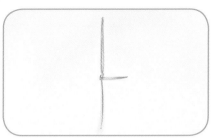

2 Cross one end of the wire over the other about 1¾ in. (4.4 cm) from the fold. Wrap the bent end around the straight wire three times. Trim the wrapping wire.

3 String a bead or spacer and make a wrapped loop (Basics). Use the notch closest to your crimping pliers' tip to pinch the wires together. Make a slight bend at the tip of the fold.

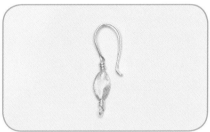

4 Use roundnose pliers to curve the loop downward, making sure the bent tip faces outward. Pair the clasp with a large soldered jump ring or a round link.

Tips

• Make folded crimps (Basics) rather than flattened crimps. Folded crimps can be hidden under large-hole spacers.
• If you don't use spacers with large holes, consider using a crimp cover to hide each crimp.

Supplies

necklace 20 in. (51 cm)
- ◆ **6** 24 mm accent beads
- ◆ 16-in. (41 cm) strand 18 mm nuggets
- ◆ **12–16** 10 mm chips
- ◆ **36–44** 4 mm large-hole spacers
- ◆ flexible beading wire, .018 or .019
- ◆ **2** crimp beads
- ◆ toggle clasp or hook clasp
- ◆ crimping pliers
- ◆ diagonal wire cutters

bracelet
- ◆ **2** 24 mm accent beads
- ◆ **5–6** 18 mm nuggets
- ◆ **6–7** 10 mm chips
- ◆ **16–18** 4 mm large-hole spacers
- ◆ flexible beading wire, .018 or .019
- ◆ **2** crimp beads
- ◆ lobster claw clasp and soldered ring
- ◆ crimping pliers
- ◆ diagonal wire cutters

earrings
- ◆ **2** 24 mm accent beads
- ◆ **2** 11º seed beads
- ◆ **4** 4 mm spacers
- ◆ 16 in. (41 cm) 18-gauge half-hard wire
- ◆ **2** 2-in. (5 cm) head pins
- ◆ pair of earring wires
- ◆ chainnose and roundnose pliers
- ◆ diagonal wire cutters

hook clasp
- ◆ 8 in. (20 cm) 18-gauge half-hard wire
- ◆ 6–12 mm large-hole bead or spacer
- ◆ chainnose and roundnose pliers
- ◆ diagonal wire cutters

Multifaceted multi

Combine an unusual gemstone cut with pearls in a five-strand necklace ◆ by Naomi Fujimoto

To embrace fall's trend of mixing jewel tones, I paired the best and brightest in gemstones: Faceted rubies and amethysts make a striking color-blocked necklace. I added tiny pearls and vermeil spacers to unify the design, and opted to wear the decorative clasp off center for maximum impact.

① bracelet •
Cut a piece of beading wire (Basics, p. 12). String nuggets interspersed with spacers and pearls until the strand is within 1 in. (2.5 cm) of the finished length. If desired, include an off-center nugget in a different color.

② On each end, attach half of a clasp (Basics).

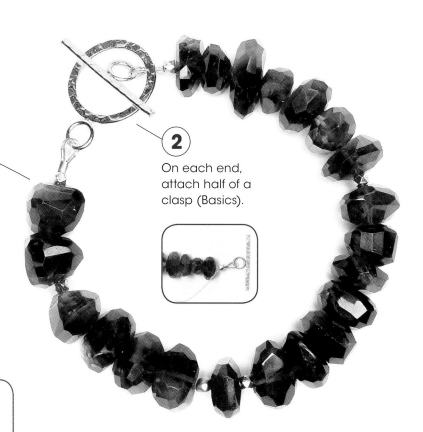

Tip
Twist the strands gently to wear the necklace. Don't twist the clasp; that puts extra stress on the finishing and can cause breakage.

❝For a pleasing combination, choose pearls in a color that works with each individual gemstone shade.❞ —NF

colored multistrand

1

necklace • Cut a piece of .014 or .015 beading wire (Basics). Center a spacer. On each end, string nuggets interspersed with spacers until the strand is within 2 in. (5 cm) of the finished length.

2

Cut four pieces of .010 beading wire. On each wire, string pearls interspersed with spacers until the strand is within 2 in. (5 cm) of the finished length. (String the pearl strands about 1 in./2.5 cm longer than the nugget strand if you want to wear the strands twisted.)

3

Attach a clasp (Technique, p. 50).

Supplies

necklace 18½ in. (47 cm)
- ◆ **2** 8-in. (20 cm) strands 11–14 mm faceted gemstone nuggets
- ◆ **4–5** 16-in. (41 cm) strands 3 mm pearls
- ◆ **35–50** 3 mm spacers
- ◆ flexible beading wire, .010
- ◆ flexible beading wire, .014 or .015
- ◆ **6** crimp beads
- ◆ **6** Wire Guardians
- ◆ three-strand box clasp
- ◆ chainnose or crimping pliers
- ◆ diagonal wire cutters

bracelet
- ◆ 8-in. (20 cm) strand 11–14 mm faceted gemstone nuggets
- ◆ **1–2** 3 mm pearls
- ◆ **5–8** 3 mm spacers
- ◆ flexible beading wire, .014 or .015
- ◆ **6** crimp beads
- ◆ **2** Wire Guardians
- ◆ toggle clasp
- ◆ chainnose or crimping pliers
- ◆ diagonal wire cutters

earrings
- ◆ **2** 10–14 mm faceted gemstone nuggets
- ◆ **2** 3 mm pearls
- ◆ **2** 35–40 mm marquise links
- ◆ **2** 1½-in. (3.8 cm) head pins
- ◆ pair of earring wires
- ◆ chainnose and roundnose pliers
- ◆ diagonal wire cutters

Technique: Finishing a multistrand necklace

1. On each end of the nugget strand, string a crimp bead, a Wire Guardian, and the middle loop of a clasp. Go back through the crimp bead and tighten the wire. Crimp the crimp bead (Basics) and trim the excess wire. Tuck the excess wire into the adjacent bead.

2. Over each pair of pearl strands, string a crimp bead, a Wire Guardian, and the corresponding loop of the clasp. Go back through the crimp bead and the pearls. Check the fit, and add or remove beads if necessary. Tighten the wires and crimp the crimp bead.

Design alternative

Try designing with color trends in mind: Some combinations that I considered are below.

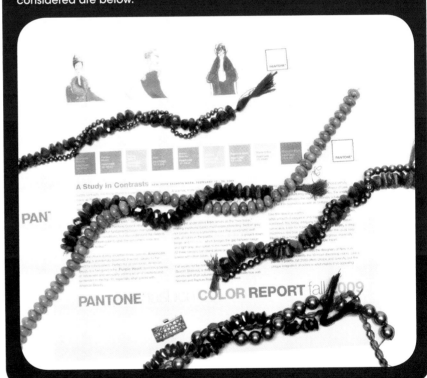

earrings • For each earring: On a head pin, string a nugget and a pearl. Make the first half of a wrapped loop (Basics). Attach a marquise link and complete the wraps. Attach the dangle and the loop of an earring wire.

A corner on STYLE

A single strand of diagonally drilled squares makes an edgy set

by Linda Aspenson Bergstrom

There's no doubt about it — the bracelet is the star of this set. Let your eyes hopscotch across the squares, cleverly arranged by stringing the wire through the beads in unexpected directions. Use the remaining squares to make a necklace and earrings with bicones and kite-shaped chandelier components that accentuate the angles of the beads.

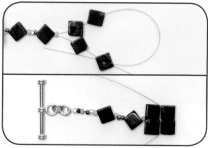

1 bracelet • Cut a 25-in. (64 cm) piece of beading wire. Center half of a clasp on the wire. Over both wires, string three seed beads and a microcrimp bead. Flatten the crimp bead (Basics, p. 12). Over both wires, string: three seed beads, square, three seed beads, square, one seed bead.

2 On each wire, string two squares. With one wire, go back through the last square on the opposite wire. Gently tighten the wire until the beads form a four-square. Repeat with the other wire.

3 On each wire, string 13 to 17 seed beads. Over both wires, string a seed bead, a square, and a seed bead. On each wire, string a square and five seed beads.

4 String the wires through a square in opposite directions. Pull the wires gently so the previous two squares sit side by side.

5 On each wire, string five seed beads and a square. Over both wires, string a seed bead, a square, and a seed bead. On each wire, string 13 to 17 seed beads.

6 On each wire, string a square. With one wire, go back through the square on the opposite wire. Repeat with the other wire. On each wire, string a square. These beads will form a four-square in step 7.

7 Over both wires, string: seed bead, square, three seed beads, square, three seed beads, standard crimp bead, three seed beads, half of a clasp. Check the fit, and add or remove beads if necessary. Go back through the last few beads strung and tighten the wires. Crimp the crimp bead and trim the excess wire. Close a crimp cover over each crimp.

1 necklace • Cut a 1¼-in. (3.2 cm) piece of wire and make a plain loop (Basics). String a 4 mm bicone crystal, a square, and a 4 mm. Make a plain loop. Make four double-bicone units.

2 Cut a 1½-in. (3.8 cm) piece of wire and make a plain loop. String a seed bead, a square, a 6 mm bicone crystal, and a seed bead. Make a plain loop. Make eight single-bicone units.

Supplies

necklace 32–33 in. (81–84 cm)
- 16-in. (41 cm) strand 6–8 mm gemstone squares, diagonally drilled
- **8** 6 mm bicone crystals
- **8** 4 mm bicone crystals
- 1 g 11º seed beads
- 33 in. (84 cm) 22-gauge half-hard wire
- 13 in. (33 cm) chain, 3–4 mm links
- chainnose and roundnose pliers
- diagonal wire cutters

bracelet
- **19** 6–8 mm gemstone squares left over from necklace
- 1–2 g 11º seed beads
- flexible beading wire, .010
- **2** crimp beads, **1** standard and **1** micro
- **2** crimp covers
- toggle clasp
- chainnose pliers
- diagonal wire cutters
- crimping pliers (optional)

earrings
- **2** 6–8 mm gemstone squares left over from necklace
- **6** 4 mm bicone crystals
- **2** 3-to-1 chandelier components
- **8** 1-in. (2.5 cm) head pins
- pair of earring wires
- chainnose and roundnose pliers
- diagonal wire cutters
- E6000 adhesive
- toothpick

Tip

To make the four-squares in the bracelet, use only squares that are the same size and drilled perfectly corner to corner.

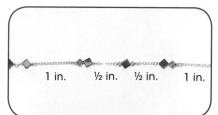

3 Cut a 1-in. (2.5 cm) piece of wire and make a plain loop. String a seed bead, a square, and a seed bead. Make a plain loop perpendicular to the first. Make 16 square units.

4 Open a loop (Basics) of a square unit and attach a loop of another square unit. Close the loop. Attach four squares to make a linked-square segment. Make four linked-square segments.

5 Cut eight ½-in. (1.3 cm) and eight 1-in. (2.5 cm) pieces of chain. Attach: linked-square segment, 1-in. chain, single-bicone unit, ½-in. chain, double-bicone unit, ½-in. chain, single-bicone unit, 1-in. chain. Continue attaching in this pattern. Attach the final chain to the first linked-square segment.

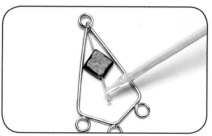

1 earrings • On a head pin, string a square. At the end of the head pin, make a plain loop (Basics). Open the loop (Basics) and attach the top loop of a chandelier component. Close the loop.

2 Slide the square up and use a toothpick to spread adhesive on the lower part of the head pin. Slide the square over the adhesive and let dry.

3 On a head pin, string a bicone crystal and make the first half of a wrapped loop (Basics). Make three bicone units.

4 Attach a bicone unit to each bottom loop of the chandelier and complete the wraps. Open the loop of an earring wire and attach the dangle. Close the loop. Make a second earring.

Tips

• Diagonally drilled squares may also be called diamonds or rhombuses, depending on where you buy them.
• For the bracelet, use a micro-crimp bead for the end with two passes of wire and a standard size crimp bead for the end with four passes of wire. Crimp covers will make both crimps look the same size.

A sleek stone or an organic slab looks gorgeous hung from a wire bail.

Making bail

Escape from traditional bails with free-form wirework

by **Alaina Burnett**

I started making wire bails because I didn't want to use store-bought components and I needed something bolder to balance my large gemstone pendants. The first few bails I made were very symmetrical and neat — that's when I decided to turn my head away as I worked so I couldn't see what I was doing. One of my favorite moments is when I get to look at the bail I just made and be surprised by how well it turned out.

1 necklace • Cut a 12-in. (30 cm) piece of 22-gauge wire. About 1 in. (2.5 cm) from one end, make a bend. Wrap the short tail loosely around the long tail.

2 String a charm and a pendant. Bend the wire up behind the pendant and wrap it loosely around the wraps made in step 1.

3 Bend the wire to make a loop parallel to the first loop and continue wrapping around the previous wraps.

4 Trim the wire to 1 in. (2.5 cm) and use roundnose pliers to make a loop. Open the loop (Basics, p. 12), wrap the wire one more time, and anchor the loop to a wrap. Close the loop.

5 Cut a piece of beading wire (Basics) and center the pendant. On each side, string beads and spacers until the strand is within 1 in. (2.5 cm) of the finished length.

6 On each end, attach half of a two-strand toggle clasp (Basics).

7 Cut a piece of beading wire 2 in. (5 cm) shorter than the first. String beads and spacers as desired until the strand is within 1 in. (2.5 cm) of the finished length. Attach the clasp.

"I always use my fingers to shape my bails. Pliers and tools are fantastic, but getting your hands involved helps make the bails unique." —AB

1 earrings • On a head pin, string beads and spacers. Make a plain loop (Basics).

2 Open the loop of an earring wire (Basics) and attach the dangle. Close the loop. Make a second earring.

Design alternative

Turn a wirework bail into a centerpiece. Make a frame of 20-gauge wire with a loop on each end, then wrap 22-gauge wire loosely around it. This technique works great for top-drilled pendants.

Supplies

necklace 19 in. (48 cm)
- 45–65 mm pendant
- **3–5** 16-in. (41 cm) strands 3–14 mm gemstone beads
- 12–18 mm charm
- **65–80** 4–6 mm spacers
- flexible beading wire, .018–.019
- 12 in. (30 cm) 22-gauge half-hard wire
- **4** crimp beads
- two-strand toggle clasp
- chainnose and roundnose pliers
- diagonal wire cutters
- crimping pliers (optional)

earrings
- **6** 3–14 mm gemstone beads left over from necklace
- **4** 4–6 mm spacers
- **2** 1½-in. (3.8 cm) head pins
- pair of earring wires
- chainnose and roundnose pliers
- diagonal wire cutters

These focal stones are turquoise and lemon chrysoprase. The necklace on page 58 highlights dyed jade and blue crackle agate.

Mix and match colored stones for drama

by Carol McKinney

Earthy statement

Many chic statement necklaces rely heavily on faux gems. If your style message is earthier, Mother Nature offers all the color you need. Choose a couple of large stones as focal points and finish your strand with smaller stones in matching or contrasting colors.

1 necklace • Cut a piece of beading wire (Basics, p. 12). On the wire, string: 8 mm round bead, 25–40 mm gemstone, 8 mm, 25–40 mm, 8 mm.

2 On one end, string 3–4 in. (7.6–10 cm) of rondelles, 10 mm rounds, and 12 mm rounds. On the other end, string rounds and rondelles until the strand is within 1 in. (2.5 cm) of the finished length.

3 On each end, string an 8 mm and attach the clasp (Basics).

4 On a head pin, string a 15–20 mm gemstone. Make the first half of a wrapped loop (Basics).

5 Attach the dangle and half of the clasp. Complete the wraps.

1 earrings • Cut a piece of chain with four long links. On a head pin, string a 10 mm round bead and make the first half of a wrapped loop (Basics). Make a bead unit with an 8 mm round bead.

2 On each end of the chain, attach a bead unit and complete the wraps. Open the loop of an earring wire (Basics) and attach the second link of the chain. Close the loop. Make a second earring to match the first.

Supplies

necklace 17 in. (43 cm)
- **2** 25–40 mm gemstones
- 15–20 mm gemstone
- **6–12** 12 mm gemstone rondelles
- **10–18** 12 mm round gemstones
- **16–24** 10 mm round gemstones
- **5** 8 mm round gemstones
- flexible beading wire, .014 or .015
- 2-in. (5 cm) head pin
- **2** crimp beads
- hook-and-eye clasp
- chainnose and roundnose pliers
- diagonal wire cutters
- crimping pliers (optional)

earrings
- **2** 10 mm round gemstones
- **2** 8 mm round gemstones
- 5 in. (13 cm) long-and-short chain, 12 and 5 mm links
- **4** 2-in. (5 cm) head pins
- pair of earring wires
- chainnose and roundnose pliers
- diagonal wire cutters

Design alternative

A multicolored, graduated strand of Soochow jade gives you a ready-made mix of shapes and colors. Instead of adding other stones, I strung copper wire components for a metallic accent.

Design note

When I was deciding on the focal pieces for the green version of this necklace, I experimented with a carved jade bead. I loved the way it looked, but in the end, I thought the necklace needed the pop of the blue wedge-shaped stone.

Briolettes
at the base

One pattern offers a variety of design options

by Jenny Van

A dozen faceted rondelles cascade from delicate chain, and sitting at the bottom is a pretty briolette. It's a classic design that you can customize by altering the length of chain, introducing larger beads, or experimenting with colors. Innumerable options will reveal themselves as you explore this simple design.

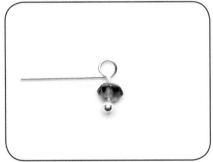

1 Cut a 3-in. (7.6 cm) piece of wire. String a briolette and make a set of wraps above it (Basics, p. 12). Make the first half of a wrapped loop (Basics) perpendicular to the briolette.

2 On a head pin, string a rondelle. Make the first half of a wrapped loop. Make 12 head pin units.

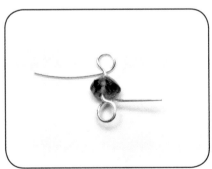

3 Cut a 2-in. (5 cm) piece of wire. Make the first half of a wrapped loop. String a rondelle and make the first half of a wrapped loop perpendicular to the first loop. Set aside for step 7.

4 Cut a seven-link piece of chain. Attach the loop of the briolette unit to one end and complete the wraps.

5 Attach two head pin units on the same end link, one on each side of the briolette unit. Complete the wraps.

6 Attach a head pin unit to each side of each link. Do not attach head pin units to the top link.

Supplies

- ◆ **2** 12 mm briolettes
- ◆ **26** 3–4 mm rondelles
- ◆ 10 in. (25 cm) 26-gauge half-hard wire
- ◆ 1½ in. (3.8 cm) chain, 2 mm links
- ◆ **24** 1-in. (2.5 cm) head pins
- ◆ pair of earring wires
- ◆ chainnose and roundnose pliers
- ◆ diagonal wire cutters

7 Attach one loop of the rondelle unit to the top link. Attach the dangle and the loop of an earring wire. Complete the wraps. Make a second earring.

Tip

To make evenly sized loops on every rondelle unit, mark the point on your roundnose pliers where you want to form the loop. (You can use rubbing alcohol to remove the mark later.)

Design alternative

Skip the chain and make a shorter pair of earrings. On a 3-in. (7.6 cm) piece of wire, string a briolette and make a set of wraps. String each rondelle unit on the wire, make a wrapped loop, and attach an earring wire.

66 Designing jewelry is a creative departure from my job as a microbiologist. 99 –JV

The broad appeal of nuggets

Get multiple pieces of jewelry from one strand of giant beads

by Jane Konkel

These shapely rutilated quartz nuggets appealed to me because they seem to glow, but any strand of large beads will work nicely for these designs. Play up the stones' charcoal-colored striations with gunmetal chain, or pair brown accents with brass. A single strand of nuggets is enough to make two necklaces, two bracelets, and a pair of earrings.

1 seven-nugget necklace • Cut two 6–10-in. (15–25 cm) pieces of chain. Set the chains aside for step 3. Cut a 13-in. (33 cm) piece of beading wire. Center a nugget.

2 On each end, string a spacer and a nugget. Repeat until the beaded section is about 6½ in. (16.5 cm) long.

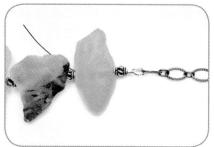

3 On each end, string a crimp bead, a Wire Guardian, and a chain. Go back through the last few beads strung and tighten the wire. Crimp the crimp bead (Basics, p. 12) and trim the excess wire.

4 Open a jump ring (Basics) and attach a hook clasp to one end. Close the jump ring. Close a crimp cover over each crimp.

"By breaking up a strand, you can make five chunky yet lightweight pieces of jewelry." –JK

Make one necklace longer than the other and layer them.

1 single-nugget necklace • On a head pin, string a nugget and make the first half of a wrapped loop (Basics).

2 Cut a 14–18-in. (36–46 cm) piece of chain. Cut the chain in half. Attach the bead unit to one end of each chain and complete the wraps.

3 Open a jump ring (Basics) and attach a lobster claw clasp and one end of the chain. On the other end, attach a jump ring.

63

1 chain bracelet • Cut a 9-in. (23 cm) piece of beading wire (Basics). String a spacer and a nugget. Repeat until the beaded section is about 3½ in. (8.9 cm). End with a spacer.

2 Cut a 6–8-in. (15–20 cm) piece of chain. On one end of the beaded strand, string a crimp bead, a Wire Guardian, and both ends of the chain. Go back through the last few beads strung and tighten the wire.

3 Repeat step 2 on the other end, substituting the loop half of a toggle clasp for the chain. On each end, crimp the crimp bead (Basics) and trim the excess wire. Close a crimp cover over each crimp.

4 Open a jump ring (Basics) and attach the chain's center link and the bar half of the toggle clasp. Close the jump ring.

1 earrings • Make a bead unit as in step 1 of the single-nugget necklace. Cut a 1½–2½-in. (3.8–6.4 cm) piece of chain. Attach the bead unit and one end of the chain. Complete the wraps.

2 Open the loop of an earring wire (Basics). Attach the dangle and close the loop. Make a second earring.

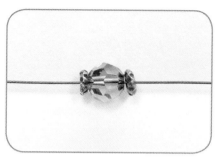

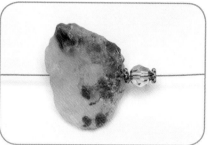

1 crystal bracelet • Cut a piece of beading wire (Basics). String a spacer, a crystal, and a spacer.

2 String a nugget, a spacer, a crystal, and a spacer. Repeat until the bracelet is within 2 in. (5 cm) of the finished length.

3 On each end, attach half of a toggle clasp (Basics).

4 Close a crimp cover over each crimp.

Supplies

seven-nugget necklace
26½ in. (67.3 cm)

- 16-in. (41 cm) strand 20–40 mm nuggets
- **8–12** 6 mm spacers
- flexible beading wire, .018 or .019
- 14–20 in. (36–51 cm) chain, 6–10 mm links
- 6 mm jump ring
- **2** crimp beads
- **2** crimp covers
- **2** Wire Guardians
- hook clasp
- chainnose and roundnose pliers, or **2** pairs of chainnose pliers
- diagonal wire cutters
- crimping pliers (optional)

single-nugget necklace
16 in. (41 cm)

- 20–40 mm nugget
- 14–18 in. (36–46 cm) chain, 3–4 mm links

- 2-in. (5 cm) head pin
- **2** 4–6 mm jump rings
- lobster claw clasp
- chainnose and roundnose pliers
- diagonal wire cutters

chain bracelet

- **3–5** 20–40 mm nuggets left over from necklace
- **8–12** 6 mm spacers
- flexible beading wire, .018 or .019
- 6–8 in. (15–20 cm) chain, 6–10 mm links
- 6 mm jump ring
- **2** crimp beads
- **2** crimp covers
- **2** Wire Guardians
- toggle clasp
- chainnose and roundnose pliers, or **2** pairs of chainnose pliers
- diagonal wire cutters
- crimping pliers (optional)

earrings

- **2** 20–40 mm nuggets left over from necklace
- 3–5 in. (7.6–13 cm) chain, 3–4 mm links
- **2** 2-in. (5 cm) head pins
- pair of earring wires
- chainnose and roundnose pliers
- diagonal wire cutters

crystal bracelet

- **7–9** 20–40 mm nuggets left over from necklace
- **7–9** 6 mm crystals
- **14–18** 4 mm spacers
- flexible beading wire, .018 or .019
- **2** crimp beads
- **2** crimp covers
- toggle clasp
- chainnose or crimping pliers
- diagonal wire cutters

Crystals

Dangle, sparkle, & shine

Glue flat-back crystals to brass components for a spark of color

by Monica Lueder

Attaching flat-back crystals to these brass components is simple — the hard part is knowing when to stop. The colors are so pretty, I always want more. To make sure I don't overdo it, I always place the crystals on the component first — without gluing — then ask myself, "Can I do without this one (or two or three)?" I usually remove at least a couple and find I have a better design.

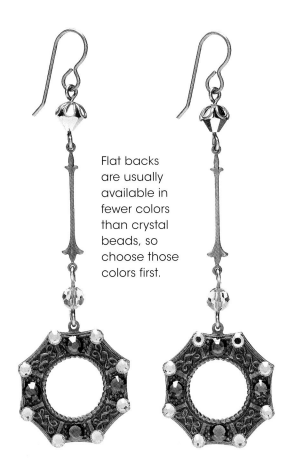

Flat backs are usually available in fewer colors than crystal beads, so choose those colors first.

1 Arrange flat-back crystals on a pendant. Mix two-part epoxy according to the package directions. Use a toothpick to apply a dot of epoxy to each flat back and the pendant. Press together and allow to dry.

2 Cut a 1-in. (2.5 cm) piece of wire. Make a plain loop (Basics, p. 12). String a 4 mm bicone crystal. Make a plain loop.

Cut a 1-in. (2.5 cm) piece of wire. Make a plain loop. String a 6 mm bicone crystal and a bead cap. Make a plain loop perpendicular to the first loop.

3 Open the loops (Basics) of the 4 mm bicone unit. Attach the pendant and a connector. Close the loops.

4 Open the loops of the 6 mm bicone unit. Attach the connector and an earring wire. Close the loops. Make a second earring.

Design alternative

If you prefer shorter earrings, omit the connectors.

Tips

• Use rubbing alcohol on a cotton swab to remove any excess epoxy before it dries.
• The brass components in this project are from Vintaj Natural Brass Co. The connectors are called "fleur de lis." The larger pendant is called "fussy peacock" and the smaller is called "Asian window."

Color notes

Fussy peacock pendants
• 6 mm bicones: Siam
• 4 mm bicones: amethyst AB
• 5 mm flat backs (SS20): volcano
• 4 mm flat backs (SS16): fuchsia
• 3 mm flat backs (SS12): sun

Asian window pendants
• 6 mm bicones: blue zircon AB
• 5 mm rounds: amethyst
• 4 mm flat backs (SS16): purple velvet
• 3 mm flat backs (SS12): blue zircon

Supplies

◆ **2** 26–31 mm round pendants
◆ **2** 25 mm connectors
◆ **2** 6 mm bicone crystals
◆ **2** 4 mm bicone crystals
◆ **4** 5 mm flat-back crystals
◆ **6** 4 mm flat-back crystals
◆ **6** 3 mm flat-back crystals
◆ **2** 6 mm blossom bead caps
◆ 4 in. (10 cm) 22-gauge half-hard wire
◆ pair of earring wires
◆ chainnose and roundnose pliers
◆ diagonal wire cutters
◆ toothpick
◆ two-part epoxy

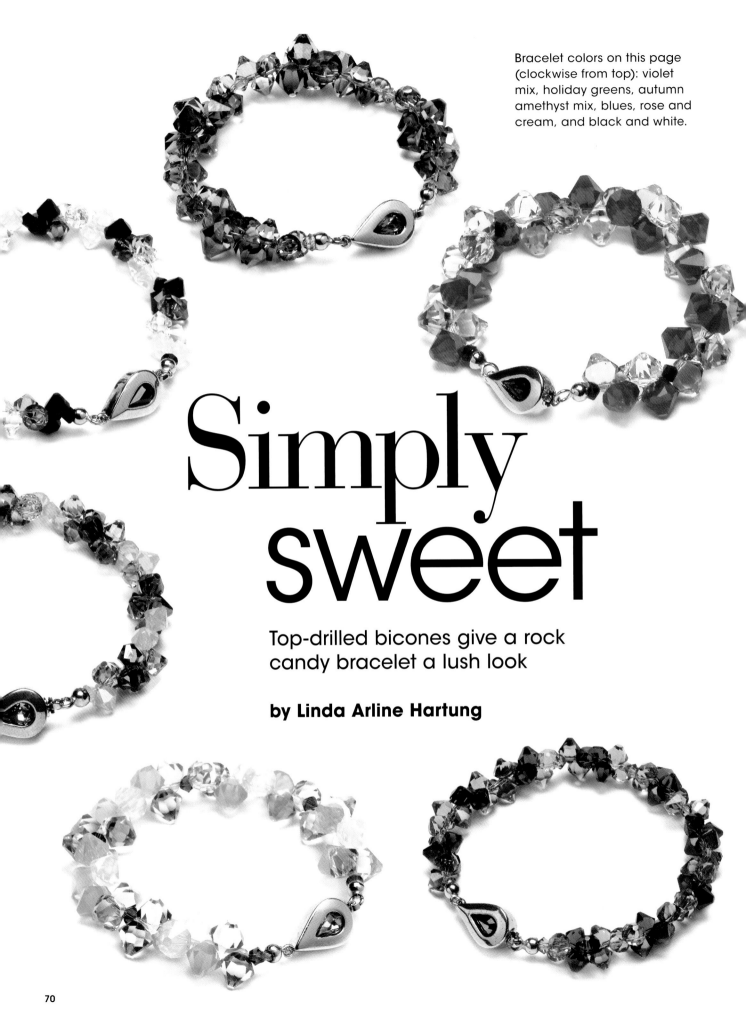

Bracelet colors on this page (clockwise from top): violet mix, holiday greens, autumn amethyst mix, blues, rose and cream, and black and white.

Simply sweet

Top-drilled bicones give a rock candy bracelet a lush look

by Linda Arline Hartung

Several years ago I bought some rock candy swizzle sticks for my espresso and they reminded me of top-drilled bicone crystals. I made a bracelet with 6 mm and 8 mm Crystallized Swarovski Elements in crystal AB (below) to duplicate the look of the candy. After that, I started experimenting with different color and size combinations. I think all of these bracelets and earrings look delicious!

1 bracelet • Cut a piece of beading wire (Basics, p. 12). On one end, string a crimp bead. Crimp the crimp bead (Basics) about 1 in. (2.5 cm) from the end. String: 4 mm bicone crystal, six top-drilled bicones, crimp bead, two top-drilled bicones, 4 mm bicone.

2 Position the six top-drilled bicones snugly between the crimp beads. Flatten the second crimp bead (Basics) as close as possible to the bicone cluster. String a pattern of eight top-drilled bicones and a 4 mm bicone, repeating until the strand is within ½ in. (1.3 cm) of the finished length.

3 Hold the strand vertically and position the top-drilled crystals so they fit together snugly. Check the fit, and add or remove beads if necessary. Remove the last seven crystals strung, string a crimp bead, and flatten it. Restring the seven crystals and string another crimp bead. Position the crystals and crimp the crimp bead.

4 On each end, trim the wire to 1 mm. Mix two-part epoxy according to the package directions. Fill a bell end-cap ¾ full of epoxy. Push the cap over an end crimp and onto the adjacent 4 mm bicone. Repeat on the other end. Wipe off the excess epoxy and let dry.

5 On each end, open the loop (Basics) of the end-cap and attach half of a clasp. Close the loop.

"This project is perfect for the beader with a sweet tooth — like me!"
–LAH

1 earrings • On a head pin, string a 4 mm bicone crystal, four to six top-drilled bicones, and a 4 mm. Make the first half of a wrapped loop (Basics).

2 Mix two-part epoxy according to the package directions. Put a small amount of epoxy in the earring post cup and insert the drilled end of a top-drilled bicone. Let dry.

3 Attach the dangle to the loop of the earring post and complete the wraps. Make a second earring.

Tips

• The flattened crimps in steps 2 and 3 are optional but strongly encouraged. Keeping the correct tension maintains the clustered look from one end of the bracelet to the other without overtightening (and breaking) the crystals.
• The teardrop clasp is sold without the crystal inset. Use two-party epoxy to adhere a #4300 (8 x 4.8 mm) Crystallized Swarovski Elements component.
• Isopropyl (rubbing) alcohol on a cotton swab will remove excess epoxy before it dries.
• Make post earrings by following earring step 2 and clipping off the loop with diagonal wire cutters.

Supplies

all bracelets
◆ **6–10** 4 mm bicone or Xilion crystals
◆ flexible beading wire, .018 or .019
◆ **4** crimp beads
◆ **2** bell end-caps
◆ teardrop clasp and crystal inset
◆ chainnose and roundnose pliers, or **2** pairs of chainnose pliers
◆ diagonal wire cutters
◆ crimping pliers (optional)
◆ two-part epoxy

8 mm-crystal bracelet
◆ **40–48** 8 mm top-drilled bicones

8 mm- and 6 mm-crystal bracelet
◆ **24–27** 8 mm top-drilled bicones
◆ **32–36** 6 mm top-drilled bicones

6 mm-crystal bracelet
◆ **63–72** 6 mm top-drilled bicones

earrings
◆ **10–14** 6 or 8 mm top-drilled bicone crystals
◆ **4** 4 mm bicone or Xilion crystals
◆ **2** 2-in. (5 cm) head pins
◆ pair of earring posts with cups, plus ear nuts
◆ chainnose and roundnose pliers
◆ diagonal wire cutters
◆ two-part epoxy

Color combinations

violet mix
• violet satin (8 mm)
• aqua satin (6 mm)
• light Colorado topaz (6 mm)
• light Colorado topaz (4 mm)

holiday greens
• palace green opal (8 mm)
• peridot (8 mm)
• jonquil (8 mm)
• dark red coral (4 mm)

autumn amethyst mix
• amethyst (6 mm)
• khaki (6 mm)
• topaz (6 mm)
• khaki (4 mm)

blues
• white opal (8 mm)
• light sapphire (8 mm)
• air blue opal (8 mm)
• aquamarine (8 mm)
• Montana (4 mm)

rose and cream
• light rose satin (6 mm)
• sand opal (6 mm)
• light Colorado topaz (6 mm)
• sand opal (4 mm)

black and white
• jet (6 mm)
• black diamond (6 mm)
• crystal (6 mm)
• white opal (6 mm)
• jet (4 mm)

Delicate
garnet

A filigree bezel holds
a garnet-colored
treasure
in this delicate
necklace

by Irina Miech

To add dimension, separate bicones with tiny seed beads. Include a chain extender for flexibility.

Supplies

necklace 17 in. (43 cm)

- 12 mm flat-back crystal or rivoli
- 10 x 20 mm filigree
- **70–80** 3 mm bicone crystals
- 1 g 13º seed beads or Charlottes
- 3 mm spacer
- flexible beading wire, .010 or .012
- 1-in. (2.5 cm) head pin
- **2** crimp beads
- lobster claw clasp
- 2 in. (5 cm) chain for extender, 4–6 mm links
- chainnose and roundnose pliers
- diagonal wire cutters
- crimping pliers (optional)

1 Use chainnose pliers to bend a filigree's corners around a flat-back crystal or rivoli. Cut a piece of beading wire (Basics, p. 12). Center the pendant on the wire.

2 On each end, string a bicone and a 13º seed bead. Repeat for 4½–5 in. (11.4–13 cm). String seed beads until the strand is within 1 in. (2.5 cm) of the finished length.

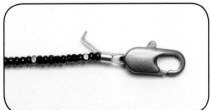

3 On one end, attach a lobster claw clasp (Basics). On the other end, attach a 2-in. (5 cm) piece of chain.

4 On a head pin, string a spacer. Make the first half of a wrapped loop (Basics) and attach the chain. Complete the wraps.

Striking
structure

Crystal components sparkle in
Art Deco statement pieces

by Cathy Jakicic

Strategically stacking double-drilled crystal components on head pins is a simple way to create the centerpiece of a traffic-stopping necklace. Using sterling silver flexible beading wire gives you the style (and budget) option of not stringing crystals all the way around.

1 necklace • String an oval crystal component on two head pins. On each head pin, string a 3 mm square tube. String two ovals over both head pins. On each head pin, string a saucer spacer, a 3 mm round spacer, and a saucer. On each head pin, make a plain loop (Basics, p. 12).

2 String an oval crystal component on two head pins. On each head pin, string a 4 mm tube. String an oval on both head pins. On each head pin, string a 3 mm round, a saucer, and a 3 mm. On each head pin, make a plain loop. Repeat to make a second shorter oval unit.

3 Cut two pieces of beading wire (Basics). On the top wire, center: saucer, 3 mm round, top hole of rose montee, 3 mm, saucer, 3 mm, top hole of rose montee, 3 mm, saucer. On the bottom wire, center: saucer, 3 mm, bottom hole of rose montee, one loop of the longer oval crystal unit, saucer, the second loop of the oval unit, bottom hole of rose montee, 3 mm, saucer.

4 On each side of the top wire, string: top hole of rectangular crystal component, 3 mm, saucer, top hole of rose montee, saucer, top hole of oval. On each side of the bottom wire, string: bottom hole of rectangle, loop of the shorter oval crystal unit, saucer, second loop of oval unit, bottom hole of rose montee, saucer, bottom hole of oval.

Supplies

necklace 18½ in. (47 cm)
- **9** 15 mm oval double-drilled silver-plated crystal components
- **4** 15 mm rectangular double-drilled silver-plated crystal components
- **6** 6 mm square rose montees
- **4** 40 x 4 mm silver-plated square tubes
- **2** 40 x 3 mm silver-plated square tubes
- **4** 4 mm round spacers
- **18** 3 mm round spacers
- **30** 3 mm saucer spacers
- sterling silver flexible beading wire, .024
- **6** 3-in. (7.6 cm) head pins
- **2** crimp tubes
- **2** bead tips, clamshell style
- toggle clasp
- chainnose and roundnose pliers
- diagonal wire cutters

bracelet
- **7–9** 15 x 5 mm marquise double-drilled silver-plated crystal components
- **8–10** 6 mm square rose montees
- **32–36** 3 mm round spacers
- sterling silver flexible beading wire, .024
- **2** crimp tubes
- **2** bead tips, clamshell style
- toggle clasp
- chainnose and roundnose pliers
- diagonal wire cutters

5 On each side of the top wire, string: saucer, top hole of rose montee, saucer, top hole of rectangle, 4 mm round spacer. On each side of the bottom wire, string: saucer, bottom hole of rose montee, saucer, bottom hole of rectangle, 4 mm.

6 Check the fit, and trim wire if necessary. On each side, over both wires, string a bead tip and a crimp tube 2 in. (5 cm) from the end of the wires. Flatten the crimp tube (Basics).

7 On each side, trim the excess wire and close the bead tip over the crimp. Attach half of a clasp and the loop of the bead tip. Close the loop.

bracelet • Cut two pieces of beading wire (Basics). String a pattern of beads and spacers until the strand is within 1½ in. (3.8 cm) of the finished length. Following necklace step 6, attach bead tips and crimp tubes ½ in. (1.3 cm) from the last bead on each end. Following step 7, attach a toggle clasp.

❝This jewelry will take the 'basic' out of a basic black dress.❞ –CJ

Design alternative
Double-drilled gemstones give an earthier feel, while flowing, delicate chain adds romance.

Crystals on curves

Embellish premade earring findings with crystals

by Christianne Camera

These sterling silver earring findings from Saki Silver make designing a breeze: Simply add a pretty arrangement of bicone and round crystals. You can also hammer the findings if you prefer a matte finish on your metals. Or, for yet another fabulous prefab option, buy square findings instead of circles.

1 On a head pin, string a bicone crystal and an 11º seed bead. Make the first half of a wrapped loop (Basics, p. 12). Make four bicone units and a round-crystal unit.

2 Attach the loop of the round-crystal unit and the soldered ring on an earring wire. Complete the wraps.

3 On each side of the round crystal, attach two bicone units. Complete the wraps as you go. Make a second earring.

Supplies

- **2** 10 mm round crystals
- **8** 4 mm bicone crystals
- **10** 11º seed beads
- **10** 1½-in. (3.8 cm) head pins
- pair of earring wires with attached ring
- chainnose and roundnose pliers
- diagonal wire cutters

A night to sparkle

Assemble a variety of crystals in a brilliant necklace and earrings
by Jenny Van

Supplies

necklace 26–31 in. (66–79 cm)
- **4** 18 mm crystal rondelles
- **7** 12 mm cosmic crystals
- **15** 6 mm helix crystals
- **9** ft. (2.7 m) 22-gauge half-hard wire
- **33–37** in. (84–94 cm) cable chain, 4 mm links
- **15–17** in. (38–43 cm) cable chain, 2 mm links
- **1½**-in. (3.8 cm) head pin
- chainnose and roundnose pliers
- diagonal wire cutters

earrings
- **2** 12 mm crystal rondelles
- **12** 4 mm round crystals
- **6** in. (15 cm) 22-gauge half-hard wire
- **20–24** in. (51–61 cm) cable chain, 2 mm links
- **12** 1½-in. (3.8 cm) head pins
- pair of earring wires
- chainnose and roundnose pliers
- diagonal wire cutters

For a holiday party, nothing beats the allure of crystals and gold. To dazzle from all angles, attach crystals and chain at the back of this clasp-less necklace (Design alternative, p. 80).

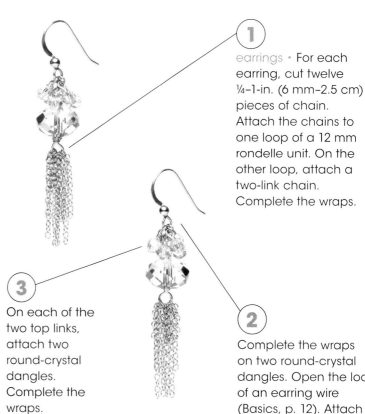

1 earrings • For each earring, cut twelve ¼–1-in. (6 mm–2.5 cm) pieces of chain. Attach the chains to one loop of a 12 mm rondelle unit. On the other loop, attach a two-link chain. Complete the wraps.

2 Complete the wraps on two round-crystal dangles. Open the loop of an earring wire (Basics, p. 12). Attach a round-crystal dangle, the top link of chain, and a round-crystal dangle. Close the loop.

3 On each of the two top links, attach two round-crystal dangles. Complete the wraps.

See p. 80 for instructions to make each component for the earrings and necklace.

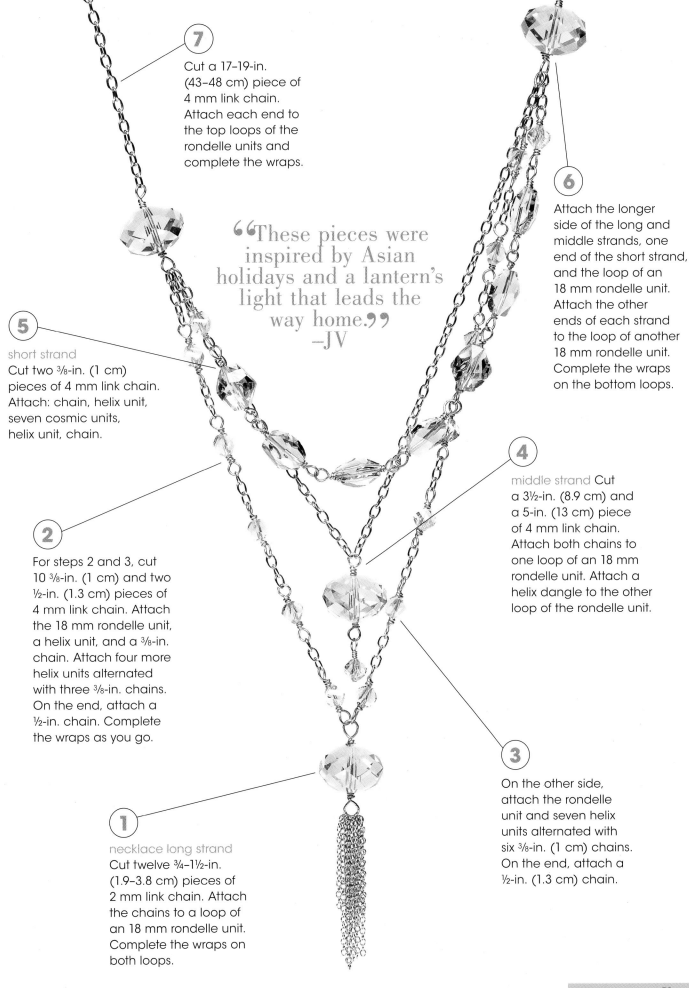

7
Cut a 17–19-in. (43–48 cm) piece of 4 mm link chain. Attach each end to the top loops of the rondelle units and complete the wraps.

"These pieces were inspired by Asian holidays and a lantern's light that leads the way home."
—JV

6
Attach the longer side of the long and middle strands, one end of the short strand, and the loop of an 18 mm rondelle unit. Attach the other ends of each strand to the loop of another 18 mm rondelle unit. Complete the wraps on the bottom loops.

5
short strand
Cut two ³⁄₈-in. (1 cm) pieces of 4 mm link chain. Attach: chain, helix unit, seven cosmic units, helix unit, chain.

4
middle strand Cut a 3½-in. (8.9 cm) and a 5-in. (13 cm) piece of 4 mm link chain. Attach both chains to one loop of an 18 mm rondelle unit. Attach a helix dangle to the other loop of the rondelle unit.

2
For steps 2 and 3, cut 10 ³⁄₈-in. (1 cm) and two ½-in. (1.3 cm) pieces of 4 mm link chain. Attach the 18 mm rondelle unit, a helix unit, and a ³⁄₈-in. chain. Attach four more helix units alternated with three ³⁄₈-in. chains. On the end, attach a ½-in. chain. Complete the wraps as you go.

3
On the other side, attach the rondelle unit and seven helix units alternated with six ³⁄₈-in. (1 cm) chains. On the end, attach a ½-in. (1.3 cm) chain.

1
necklace long strand
Cut twelve ¾–1½-in. (1.9–3.8 cm) pieces of 2 mm link chain. Attach the chains to a loop of an 18 mm rondelle unit. Complete the wraps on both loops.

Components

rondelle unit · Cut a 3½-in. (8.9 cm) piece of wire. On one end, make the first half of a wrapped loop (Basics). String a rondelle and make the first half of a wrapped loop. Make four 18 mm rondelle units for the necklace and two 12 mm rondelle units for the earrings.

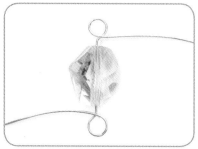

cosmic unit · Cut a 3-in. (7.6 cm) piece of wire. On one end, make the first half of a wrapped loop. String a cosmic crystal and make the first half of a wrapped loop. Make seven cosmic units for the necklace.

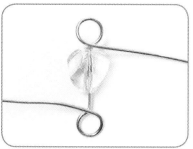

helix unit · Cut a 3-in. (7.6 cm) piece of wire. On one end, make the first half of a wrapped loop. String a helix crystal and make the first half of a wrapped loop. Make 14 helix units for the necklace.

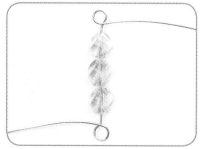

three-helix unit (optional, see Design alternative) · Cut a 3½-in. (8.9 cm) piece of wire. On one end, make the first half of a wrapped loop. String three helix crystals and make the first half of a wrapped loop. Make five three-helix units for the necklace.

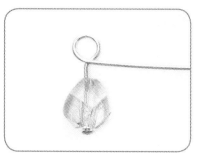

helix dangle · On a head pin, string a helix crystal and make the first half of a wrapped loop. Make one helix dangle for the necklace.

round-crystal dangle · On a head pin, string a round crystal and make the first half of a wrapped loop. Make 12 round-crystal dangles for the earrings.

Design alternative

For a more decorative finish, make four helix units and five three-helix units. In step 7, do not cut one long piece of chain. Instead, cut eight ³⁄₈-in. (1 cm) pieces of 4 mm link chain. Attach a three-helix unit, a chain, a helix unit, and a chain. Repeat four times, then attach a three-helix unit and a 4-in. (10 cm) chain.

Tip

When shopping for crystals online, look for a site that allows you to browse crystals by size or shape.

Crystal frame lariat

A sparkling lariat requires only two kinds of crystals

by Catherine Hodge

This monochromatic lariat is gorgeous with the season's moody grey-and-blue palette, but you can dress your version up or down by trying different combinations of chain and crystals. Because it's so quick and easy to make, this lariat is perfect for the holidays — as an accessory or a gift.

1 On a head pin, string a round crystal. Make the first half of a wrapped loop (Basics, p. 12). Make 15 crystal units.

2 Decide how long you want your lariat to be and cut a piece of chain to that length. On one end, attach a crystal unit. Complete the wraps.

3 Attach a crystal unit to each adjacent link, completing the wraps as you go.

4 Open a jump ring (Basics) and attach a square ring and the other end of the chain. Close the jump ring.

66 This is a great way to use a square ring component in an upscale crystal design. 99 –CH

Design alternative

For a colorful option, use round crystals in a variety of shades. You can also use a different ring shape (I used a 22 mm oval) — just make sure the opening accommodates the cluster of 6 mm crystals.

Supplies

lariat 23 in. (58 cm)

- 20 mm square crystal ring
- **15** 6 mm round crystals
- 22–26 in. (56–66 cm) chain, 3 mm links
- **15** 1½-in. (3.8 cm) head pins
- 9–10 mm jump ring
- chainnose and roundnose pliers
- diagonal wire cutters

Use crystal components
to experiment
with trends

by Theresa Drake Abelew

color
com

necklace • Cut a piece of chain to the finished length. Use a jump ring (Basics, p. 12) to attach a large rectangle to the center of the chain. Leaving ½ in. (1.3 cm) between components, attach the others as shown.

1

2

Use jump rings to attach a spring ring clasp and a soldered jump ring to the ends of the chain.

Twice a year, Swarovski releases Crystallized color mixes that reflect color trends while creating new palettes. I combined some colors from the Radiance and Emotion groups in the gold and violet necklace and earrings, and combined all the colors from the Emotion group for a matching bracelet. For a second necklace-and-earrings set, I simply used colors I like to create a personal palette.

binations

bracelet •
Use jump rings (Basics) to attach an oval component to every fourth loop of a bangle.

1

2

On each head pin, string crystals and make the first half of a wrapped loop (Basics). Attach the bangle's loops and complete the wraps.

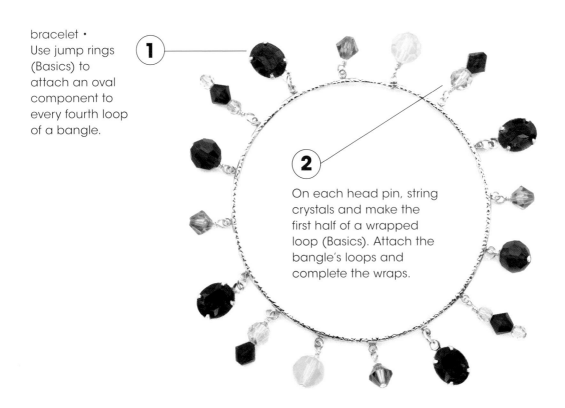

Emotion
Inspired by: intangibility, imagination, the magical

Pacific opal

crystal golden shadow

light smoked topaz

vintage rose

amethyst

dark indigo

hyacinth

mocca

Radiance
Inspired by: inner strength, clarity, balance of intellect and emotion

turquoise

smoky quartz

mocca

light Colorado topaz

crystal copper

light amethyst

white opal

smoked topaz

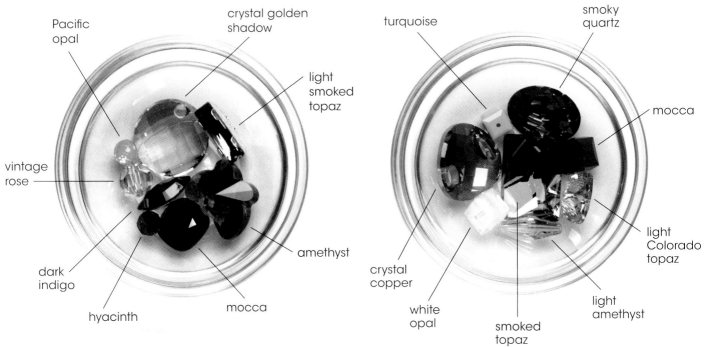

1 earrings • Cut a 3-in. (7.6 cm) piece of wire. String a two-hole component and make a set of wraps above it (Basics).

2 Make a wrapped loop above the wraps (Basics). Open a jump ring (Basics) and attach an oval component. Close the jump ring. Attach an earring wire. Make a second earring.

For quick-as-a-blink earrings, just attach a component to an earring wire.

Supplies

necklace 17 in. (43 cm)
- components
  - **3** 21 mm rectangle crystal components with loop
  - **2** 21 mm oval crystal components with loop
  - **2** 15 mm rectangle crystal components with loop
  - **2** 15 mm oval crystal components with loop
  - **4** 10 mm oval crystal components with loop
- 17–19 in. (43–48 cm) cable chain, 3–4 mm links
- **15** 4 mm jump rings
- spring ring clasp and soldered jump ring

- chainnose and roundnose pliers
- diagonal wire cutters

bracelet
- **4** 10 mm oval crystal components with loop
- **4** 8 mm round crystals
- **8** 6 mm bicone crystals
- **2** 6 mm round crystals
- **4** 4 mm round crystals
- 16-loop bangle
- **12** 2-in. (5 cm) head pins
- **4** 4 mm jump rings
- chainnose and roundnose pliers
- diagonal wire cutters

two-component earrings
- **2** 15 mm two-hole rectangle crystal components
- **2** 10 mm oval crystal components with loop
- 6 in. (15 cm) 22-gauge half-hard wire
- **2** 4 mm jump rings
- pair of earring wires
- chainnose and roundnose pliers
- diagonal wire cutters

Rich, textured foliage

Sculpt lush ferns with chocolate-colored WireLace vines and crystal leaves and branches

by Linda Arline Hartung

When I pick up my mail, I walk by our mossy rock wall covered with elegant ferns, twisted vines, and sprouts of redwoods. I love looking at the textures and colors — vibrant green fronds, grey rough-textured stone, with brown creepers and pieces of bark and branches tucked into the wall's crevices. When I looked for inspiration for this necklace, this picture immediately came to mind. I created ferns with olivine crystals and twisted WireLace-covered wire to create tendrils.

1 Cut 10 ft. (3 m) of WireLace. Cut 6 ft. (1.8 m) of 22-gauge wire and fold over 1 in. (2.5 cm) at one end. String the WireLace over the folded end to cover the entire wire, gathering the WireLace as you go.

2 On one end, twist the WireLace around the wire. Over the wire/WireLace, string an orchid pendant, an 18 mm center-drilled aquiline bead, two 18 mm top-drilled aquiline beads, and four 30 mm lily pendants.

Supplies

necklace 17 in. (43 cm)
- 40 mm crystal coral pendant
- 34 mm crystal coral pendant
- 30 mm crystal coral pendant
- **7** 30 mm crystal lily pendants
- **2** 20 mm crystal orchid pendants
- **4** 18 mm aquiline crystals, top drilled
- **2** 18 mm aquiline crystals, center drilled
- 13 ft. (4 m) 22-gauge color-coated wire
- 20 ft. (6.1 m) 2.5 mm WireLace
- leaf-shaped box clasp
- chainnose and roundnose pliers
- diagonal wire cutters
- G-S Hypo Cement
- scissors

3 Slide the crystals to the center of the wire/WireLace. Gently adjust the WireLace so it is evenly distributed on both ends of the wire. Using the side without crystals, make a wrap above the orchid. Slide down the next crystal. Make part of a second wrap and bring the wire across the second crystal.

4 Make a wrap snugly against the second crystal. Slide down the next crystal as shown. Make a second full wrap and then bring the wire across the third crystal. Be sure to keep slack in the WireLace as you wrap.

"Living among the redwoods with lush foliage year-round provides a constant source of inspiration for designing."
—LAH

5 Repeat step 4 with the remaining crystals, reversing the direction of each crystal. Make two full wraps next to the last crystal. With chainnose pliers, squeeze the wire/WireLace between crystals to align them and flatten the wraps.

6 Over one end of the wire/WireLace, string the 30 mm and 34 mm coral pendants. Slide the coral pendants 1½ in. (3.8 cm) and 2½ in. (6.4 cm) from the last lily pendant.

7 With your fingers, curve the wire/WireLace into vines. Continue free-form shaping and loosely twisting the wire/WireLace, stopping at the desired length of the necklace, and allowing 1 in. (2.5 cm) for the clasp.

8 Repeat steps 1 to 7 to make a second fern with the following substitutions: In step 2, string three 30 mm lilies instead of four. In step 6, string a 40 mm coral pendant (instead of the 30 and 34 mm pendants) 3 in. (7.6 cm) from the last lily pendant.

Attach the tongue half of the clasp between the coral pendants on fern 1 (see step 9 for instructions).

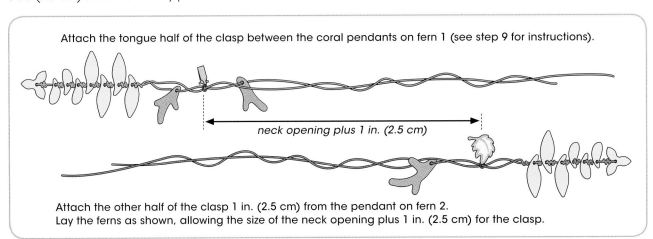

neck opening plus 1 in. (2.5 cm)

Attach the other half of the clasp 1 in. (2.5 cm) from the pendant on fern 2.
Lay the ferns as shown, allowing the size of the neck opening plus 1 in. (2.5 cm) for the clasp.

9 Cut a 6-in. (15 cm) piece of wire. On the wire, center the tongue of the clasp and make a set of wraps above it (Basics, p. 12) but do not trim the wrapping wire. Wrap each wire end three times around the fern and trim the excess wire. Repeat on the second fern with the leaf half of the clasp.

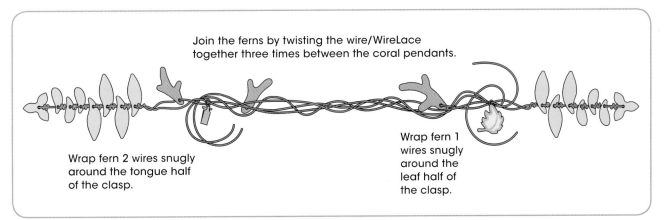

Join the ferns by twisting the wire/WireLace
together three times between the coral pendants.

Wrap fern 2 wires snugly
around the tongue half
of the clasp.

Wrap fern 1
wires snugly
around the
leaf half of
the clasp.

10 Connect the ferns and secure the wire ends as shown above. Gently bring both halves of the clasp together, shaping the wires to circle the neck.

11 Allowing for some slack, slide the excess WireLace to the end of the wires. On each end of each wire, approximately 3 in. (7.6 cm) from the clasp, twist the WireLace on the wire for about ½ in. (1.3 cm). Saturate the twisted area with glue and let dry. Trim the excess wire at the glued area.

12 On each glued end of the wire/WireLace, use roundnose pliers to create a tight coil. Pull the end of each coil to create tendrils.

13 Shape the tendrils and vines as desired. See the illustration at right for suggestions.

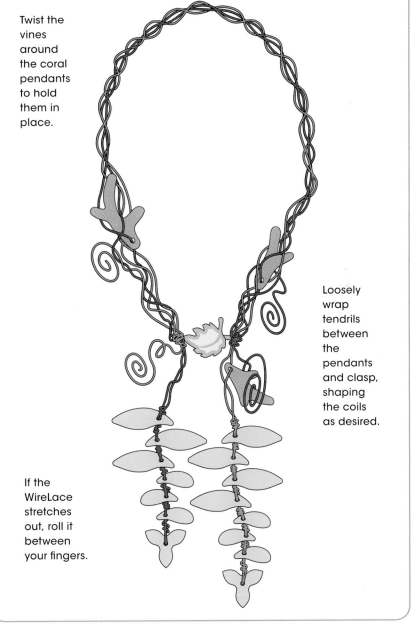

Twist the vines around the coral pendants to hold them in place.

Loosely wrap tendrils between the pendants and clasp, shaping the coils as desired.

If the WireLace stretches out, roll it between your fingers.

14 Bend the wire/WireLace to adjust fern 1 so that the top lily pendant aligns with the second lily pendant on fern 2.

Colors of
the prairie

A jewelry set evokes memories
of Circle City

by Katie Hacker

Channel-set
components
provide a
framework for
your designs.

While pondering the view from my Keystone, Ind., home, I designed this necklace and bracelet. The colors remind me of the grass and wheat below a summer sky. Indianapolis was once called Circle City, so this set has a fun connection to my birthplace, too.

1 necklace • Cut a 4-in. (10 cm) piece of beading wire. String 23 4 mm helix crystals. String one end through the beads in the opposite direction, pulling the ends to form a circle. Place the circle in the outside channel of a double-circle component.

2 Cut a 3-in. (7.6 cm) piece of wire. String 14 4 mm round crystals. Make a circle of beads as in step 1. Place the circle in the inside channel of the double-circle component.

3 On a decorative head pin, string an 8 mm helix crystal. String the holes of the circle component, making sure the head pin is on top of the wires. Make a wrapped loop (Basics, p. 12). Trim the wire tails. Cut a 12-in. (30 cm) piece of beading wire. Center the pendant.

4 On a decorative head pin, string a crystal. Make a wrapped loop. Make 12 6 mm helix units, 12 6 mm round units, 12 6 mm rondelle units, and 24 4 mm round units.

5 On each end of the wire, string: round pearl, 4 mm round unit, 6 mm helix unit, 6 mm round unit, 6 mm rondelle unit, 4 mm round unit. Repeat five times.

Tips

• Make sure you use 4 mm crystals to fill the circle components. Slightly larger crystals will not fit. You can also use round crystals instead of helix crystals.
• You can use an EZ Crimp toggle clasp finding to finish the bracelet.

• If there's a gap in the wire, close an extra crimp cover next to the first to cover it.

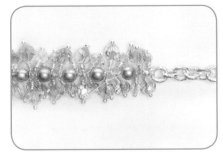

6 Cut two 6–8-in. (15–20 cm) pieces of chain. On each end of the beaded strand, string a crimp bead and a chain. Go back through the last few beads strung and tighten the wire. Crimp the crimp bead (Basics) and trim the excess wire.

7 Close a crimp cover over each crimp. On one end of the chain, open a link (Basics) and attach a lobster claw clasp. Close the link.

Supplies

necklace 17 in. (43 cm)
- 35 mm Katiedids double-circle component (katiehacker.com)
- 8 mm helix crystal
- **12** 6 mm helix crystals
- **23** 4 mm helix crystals
- **12** 6 mm crystal rondelles
- **12** 6 mm round crystals
- **38** 4 mm round crystals
- **12** 6 mm round pearls
- flexible beading wire, .014 or .015
- 12–16 in. (30–41 cm) chain, 5–7 mm links
- **61** 2-in. (5 cm) decorative head pins
- **2** crimp beads

- **2** crimp covers
- lobster claw clasp
- chainnose and roundnose pliers
- crimping pliers
- diagonal wire cutters

bracelet
- **3** 25 mm Katiedids single-circle components
- **8–12** 8 mm round pearls
- **3** 8 mm helix crystals, in **3** colors
- **14** 4 mm helix crystals
- **28** 4 mm round crystals, in **2** colors

- **10–14** 5 mm spacers
- flexible beading wire, .014 or .015
- **2** crimp beads
- **2** crimp covers
- toggle clasp
- crimping pliers
- diagonal wire cutters

1 bracelet · Following step 2 of the necklace, make a circle of 4 mm round crystals. Place the circle in the channel of a single-circle component. Make another round-crystal component and a 4 mm helix-crystal component.

Cut a piece of beading wire (Basics). Center: round pearl, hole of the helix-crystal component, spacer, 8 mm helix crystal, spacer, second hole of the component, pearl.

2 On each end, string: hole of a round-crystal component, spacer, 8 mm helix crystal, spacer, second hole of the component. String alternating pearls and spacers until the strand is within 1 in. (2.5 cm) of the finished length.

3 On each end, attach half of a toggle clasp (Basics). Close a crimp cover over each crimp.

Gold chain and
crystal components
are perfect for your
next seasonal soirée

by Liisa Turunen

Holiday charm

When you receive an invitation to a party, what are you going to wear? This necklace-and-earrings set answers the call beautifully. Channel-set crystal charms and faceted pendants will catch the glimmer of twinkling lights, and the gold components will brighten up any little black dress. Need a gift for the hostess? Whip up a second set (in less than an hour!) and you're good to go.

Supplies

necklace 16-18 in. (41-46 cm)
- **2** 18 mm crystal twist pendants
- **42** 6 mm crystal channel charms
- **22-24 in. (56-61 cm)** chain, 5 mm links
- **13** 5-6 mm jump rings
- toggle clasp
- **2** pairs of pliers (chainnose, roundnose, and/or bentnose)
- diagonal wire cutters

earrings
- **18** 6 mm crystal channel charms
- **3½ in. (8.9 cm)** chain, 5 mm links
- **4** 5-6 mm jump rings
- pair of earring wires
- **2** pairs of pliers (chainnose, roundnose, and/or bentnose)
- diagonal wire cutters

1 necklace • Cut a 3½-in. (8.9 cm) piece of chain. Open a jump ring (Basics, p. 12) and attach three channel charms, a crystal twist pendant, three charms, and one end of the chain. Close the jump ring.

2 Cut a 2-in. (5 cm) piece of chain and repeat step 1. Use jump rings to attach two sets of three charms to the chain.

Tip

The Crystallized Swarovski colors used are light Colorado topaz for the channel charms and golden shadow for the twist pendants.

3 Decide how long you want your necklace to be and cut a piece of chain to that length. Use a jump ring to attach the center link of the necklace chain, two charms, the dangles from steps 1 and 2, and two charms.

4 On each side of the dangles, use jump rings to attach three groups of three charms.

5 On one end, use a jump ring to attach the bar half of a toggle clasp. On the other end, use a jump ring to attach the loop half and two charms.

1 **earrings** • Open a jump ring (Basics) and attach three channel charms. Close the jump ring. Open a second jump ring and attach six charms. Close the jump ring.

2 Cut a 1½-in. (3.8 cm) piece of chain. Attach the six-charm jump ring to the end link. Attach the three-charm jump ring to the seventh link.

3 Open the loop of an earring wire (Basics) and attach the dangle. Make a second earring.

Design alternative

For festive earrings to wear to a special occasion, dangle channel charms in a rainbow of colors from folded silver chain.

❝I was inspired by these channel charms. They just hung so nicely and I wanted to make something fun and quick.**❞** —LT

String a
crystal sonn

Lines of crystal chain read beautifully around your neck

by Linda Arline Hartung

These necklaces go together like verses in a poem, but, like great stanzas, each is just as lovely on its own. The shorter three-strand necklace features a crystal-encrusted clasp that can be worn as a focal piece in front. Layer a second adjustable crystal chain over the shorter necklace to end with a flourish of color. Whether you make one or two pairs of earrings to finish the look, this set is much faster and easier to put together than your high school poetry assignments!

4

Repeat step 3 on the next link. Make sure to attach the briolette and teardrop units on alternate sides as shown.

3

Use a 4 mm jump ring to attach a briolette and the next ring in the chain. Use a 6 mm jump ring to attach a 16 mm teardrop and the ring.

2

Use a 4 mm jump ring to attach a briolette and the 6 mm jump ring. Use a 6 mm jump ring to attach a 16 mm teardrop and the jump ring.

1

Make a teardrop pendant with bail (Technique, p. 98). Use a 6 mm jump ring (Basics, p. 12) to attach the teardrop unit to the remaining end of the chain.

❝I wanted to make something elegant, versatile, and feminine — something I could layer and that would go from day to evening, casual to dressy.**❞** –LAH

et

three-strand necklace

1 Mix two-part epoxy and apply a layer of glue to the clasp. Set the button in the clasp and allow to dry.

2 Cut a 16-in. (41 cm) piece of chain. Cut a second piece one link longer than the first. Cut a third piece two links longer than the first. Make sure each chain begins and ends with a crystal link (not a ring).

3 Use a jump ring to attach each end of a chain to each side of the clasp. Repeat with the remaining chains, attaching them in graduating length to the clasp's corresponding loops.

Y-necklace

1 Cut a 22-in. (56 cm) piece of chain. Make sure the chain ends with a crystal link on one end and a ring on the other. Open a 4 mm jump ring (Basics, p. 12) to attach a lobster claw clasp and the end crystal link. Close the jump ring.

2 Attach the dangles as shown in the inset on page 98.

Tip

If you have bentnose pliers, use them to grip the loop in the final step in making the pendant bail. If you're new to wire wrapping, the bentnose pliers may be more comfortable to use.

Technique: Teardrop pendant with bail

1. On a crystal head pin, string a 22 mm teardrop pendant. Leaving ⅛ in. (3 mm) between the head of the head pin and the teardrop, bend the wire upward. About ⅛ in. (3 mm) above the top of the teardrop, bend the wire back at a 45-degree angle.

2. Place the jaws of your roundnose pliers above the bend and pull the wire over your pliers to create a curve.

3. Reposition the jaw of your pliers to the other side of the curve. Squeeze and rotate the pliers to complete the loop. Bend the wire tail away from the pendant.

4. Holding the base of the loop with one set of pliers, wrap the wire a little more than one full rotation behind the head of the head pin. Trim the excess wire.

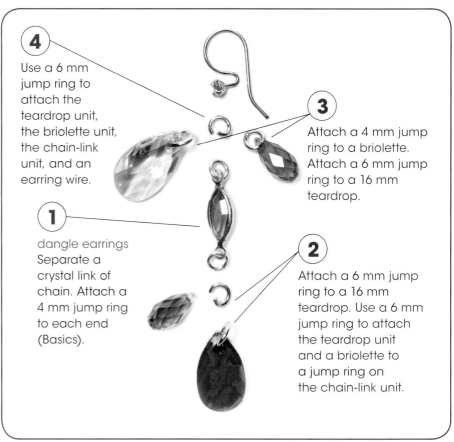

4 Use a 6 mm jump ring to attach the teardrop unit, the briolette unit, the chain-link unit, and an earring wire.

1 dangle earrings
Separate a crystal link of chain. Attach a 4 mm jump ring to each end (Basics).

3 Attach a 4 mm jump ring to a briolette. Attach a 6 mm jump ring to a 16 mm teardrop.

2 Attach a 6 mm jump ring to a 16 mm teardrop. Use a 6 mm jump ring to attach the teardrop unit and a briolette to a jump ring on the chain-link unit.

clip-on earrings
Mix two-part epoxy and apply a layer of glue to the clip-on earring finding. Set the button in the earring and allow to dry.

Color notes

• Pink necklaces/dangle earrings:
The crystal links in the chain are
fuchsia, padparadscha, rose,
light peach, and rose water opal.
The briolettes are padparadscha,
the 16 mm teardrops are ruby
and light rose, and the 22 mm
teardrop is ruby.

• Button earrings: The crystal
colors are fuchsia, light peach,
padparadscha, and rose.

• Purple necklace/earrings
(below): The crystal links in the
chain are amethyst, purple
velvet, tanzanite, and violet.
The briolettes are tanzanite,
the 24 mm and 18 mm De Art
pendants are amethyst, and the
14 mm De Art pendants are violet.

Tip

• If you use a different clasp for
the three-strand necklace, you
may have to adjust the chain
lengths. An alternate clasp can
make the graduated chains hang
differently.

Supplies

**three-strand necklace
17 in. (43 cm)**

◆ 16 mm three-tier crystal button
◆ 50 in. (1.3 m) navette crystal
  chain, 10 x 5 mm links
◆ **6** 4 mm jump rings
◆ rotunda clasp
◆ chainnose and roundnose pliers,
  or **2** pairs of chainnose pliers
◆ diagonal wire cutters
◆ two-part epoxy

Y-necklace 22 in. (56 cm)

◆ 22 mm teardrop pendant
◆ **3** 16 mm teardrop pendants
◆ **3** 11 x 5 mm briolettes
◆ 22 in. (56 cm) navette crystal
  chain, 10 x 5 mm links
◆ 1½-in. (3.8 cm) crystal head pin
◆ **4** 6 mm jump rings
◆ **4** 4 mm jump rings
◆ lobster claw clasp
◆ chainnose and roundnose pliers
◆ diagonal wire cutters

dangle earrings

◆ **4** 16 mm teardrop pendants
◆ **4** 11 x 5 mm briolettes
◆ 2 in. (5 cm) navette crystal
  chain, 10 x 5 mm links
◆ **4** 6 mm jump rings
◆ **10** 4 mm jump rings
◆ pair of crystal earring wires
◆ chainnose and roundnose pliers,
  or **2** pairs of chainnose pliers
◆ diagonal wire cutters

clip-on earrings

◆ **2** 16 mm three-tier crystal buttons
◆ pair of rotunda clip-on earrings
◆ two-part epoxy

Design alternative

Something as simple as changing the shape and color of the crystals (see
color notes for colors and shapes) can give the necklace a more edgy look.

Take a
sparkly
plunge

Waves of crystals
capture the foamy
Atlantic tides

**by Jess DiMeo
and Leah Hanoud**

This dripping sand-castle-inspired necklace-and-earrings set uses starfish and crystals with a sprinkling of pearls to convey the kinetic beauty of the tumbling waves on the beach and the sparkle of the sun on the sea. While there seems to be as many elements to the design as grains of sand on the beach, the finished necklace is well worth the time.

1 necklace • **A units:** On a decorative head pin, string a 4 mm bicone crystal. Make the first half of a wrapped loop (Basics, p. 12). Make 260 to 275 bicone units **(4 mm A)**. Make 10 to 15 more, substituting a 3 mm bicone for the 4 mm **(3 mm A)**. Make 10 to 15 more, substituting a 4 mm pearl for the bicone **(pearl A)**.

2 **B pendants:** Cut a 3-in. (7.6 cm) piece of 20-gauge wire. String a 28 mm starfish pendant and make a set of wraps above it (Basics). Make the first half of a wrapped loop perpendicular to the pendant. Make three more starfish units with 16 mm pendants **(16 mm B)**.

3 **C and D connectors:** Cut a 2-in. (5 cm) piece of 26-gauge wire. Make the first half of a wrapped loop, string a 3 mm bicone, and make the first half of a wrapped loop. Make 71 3 mm bicone connectors **(3 mm C)**. Make two 4 mm bicone connectors **(4 mm C)**. Make nine 4 mm pearl connectors **(pearl C)**. Make three additional pearl connectors using 3-in. (7.6 cm) pieces of wire for extra wrapping **(pearl D)**.

4 Cut an 18–20-in. (46–51 cm) piece of chain. Attach the 28 mm pendant to the center link and complete the wraps. Attach bead units, pendants, connectors, and chains as shown below, completing the wraps as you go.

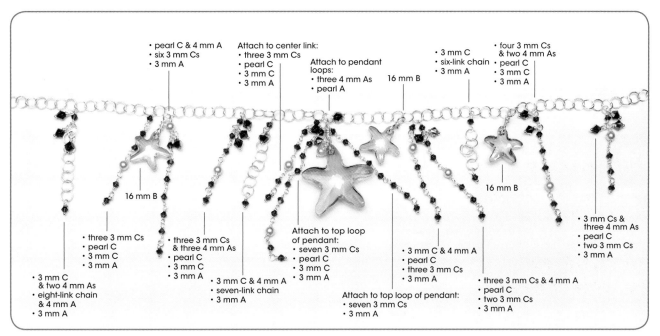

- pearl C & 4 mm A
- six 3 mm Cs
- 3 mm A

Attach to center link:
- three 3 mm Cs
- pearl C
- 3 mm C
- 3 mm A

Attach to pendant loops:
- three 4 mm As
- pearl A

16 mm B

- 3 mm C
- six-link chain
- 3 mm A

- four 3 mm Cs & two 4 mm As
- pearl C
- 3 mm C
- 3 mm A

16 mm B

16 mm B

16 mm B

- three 3 mm Cs
- pearl C
- 3 mm C
- 3 mm A

- three 3 mm Cs & three 4 mm As
- pearl C
- 3 mm C
- 3 mm A

- 3 mm C & 4 mm A
- seven-link chain
- 3 mm A

Attach to top loop of pendant:
- seven 3 mm Cs
- pearl C
- 3 mm C
- 3 mm A

- 3 mm C & 4 mm A
- pearl C
- three 3 mm Cs
- 3 mm A

- three 3 mm Cs & 4 mm A
- pearl C
- two 3 mm Cs
- 3 mm A

- 3 mm Cs & three 4 mm As
- pearl C
- two 3 mm Cs
- 3 mm A

- 3 mm C & two 4 mm As
- eight-link chain & 4 mm A
- 3 mm A

Attach to top loop of pendant:
- seven 3 mm Cs
- 3 mm A

5 Attach two **4 mm A** or **pearl A** units to each link of the chain, completing the wraps as you go. On the links that already have multiple dangles, attach only one unit.

6 Cut a 3-in. (7.6 cm) piece of chain. Attach two **4 mm A** or **pearl A** units to each link. Use the two **4 mm C** connectors to attach the end links of the short chain about 2½ in. (6.4 cm) from the center starfish on the long chain. On each end, attach two **4 mm A** units to the wrapped loop attaching the short chain.

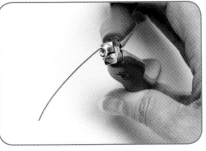

7 To make a hook clasp: Cut a 3-in. (7.6 cm) piece of 20-gauge wire. Use roundnose pliers to make a loop at the end of the wire.

8 Wrap the wire around a pen to make a hook. Trim any excess wire.

9 Gently hammer each side of the hook and a 7 mm soldered jump ring.

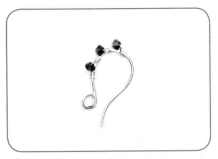

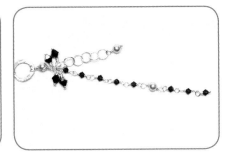

10 Cut a 3-in. (7.6 cm) piece of 26-gauge wire. Wrap the wire three times around the hook near the coil. String a 3 mm bicone and wrap the wire once or twice around the hook. Attach two more bicones, make two or three wraps, and trim the excess wire.

11 On one end, use a **pearl D** connector to attach the soldered jump ring and the chain. With the wire, make two wraps on one side of the pearl, coil the wire around the pearl, and make two more wraps. Repeat on the other end, substituting the hook clasp for the jump ring.

12 Use a **pearl D** connector to attach a six-link chain and nine remaining connectors to the jump ring as shown. Attach two **4 mm A** units to the top of each dangle and a **pearl A** to the end of the chain.

Supplies

necklace 18 in. (46 cm)
- 28 mm crystal starfish pendant
- **3** 16 mm crystal starfish pendants
- **275–300** 4 mm bicone crystals
- **30–40** 4 mm round or center-drilled rice pearls
- **65–80** 3 mm bicone crystals
- 15 in. (38 cm) 20-gauge half-hard wire
- 5 yd. (4.6 m) 26-gauge half-hard wire
- 25–27 in. (64–69 cm) round-link chain, 5.3 mm links
- **295–320** 1½-in. (3.8 cm) decorative head pins
- 7 mm soldered jump ring
- chainnose and roundnose pliers
- diagonal wire cutters
- hammer
- bench block or anvil
- pen or other cylindrical object

earrings
- **2** 16 mm crystal starfish pendants
- **14** 4 mm bicone crystals
- **6** 4 mm round or center-drilled rice pearls
- **14** 3 mm bicone crystals
- 38 in. (97 cm) 26-gauge half-hard wire
- 3 in. (7.6 cm) round-link chain, 5.3 mm links
- **14** 2-in. (5 cm) decorative head pins
- **4** 5 mm jump rings
- pair of earring wires
- chainnose and roundnose pliers
- diagonal wire cutters

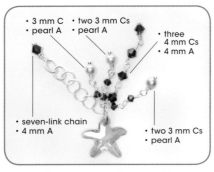

• 3 mm C
• pearl A

• two 3 mm Cs
• pearl A

• three 4 mm Cs
• 4 mm A

• seven-link chain
• 4 mm A

• two 3 mm Cs
• pearl A

1 earrings • Following necklace steps 1, 2, and 3, make two **4 mm A** units, three **pearl A** units, three **4 mm C** connectors, and five **3 mm C** connectors. Open a 5 mm jump ring (Basics, p. 12). Attach a 16 mm starfish pendant and five dangles as shown. Close the jump ring.

3 Following necklace step 10, wrap an earring wire with three 3 mm bicones. Open the loop of the earring wire (Basics) and attach the dangle. Close the loop. Make a second earring.

2 Following necklace step 1, make two **4 mm A** units. Complete the wraps. Use a jump ring to attach the starfish dangle and the A units.

Tips

• If you don't want to make your own clasp, you can still add crystal wraps to brighten a purchased hook-and-eye clasp.
• If you're skilled at wrapped loops, cut 1½-in. (3.8 cm) pieces of wire for most of the bead units and connectors.
• If desired, use 22-gauge wire to attach the pendants.

"Although the necklace looks very complex, it is actually a combination of simple techniques with a complex design.**"**
–JD and LH

Crystal rhythms

String a necklace with three distinct but harmonious design tempos

by Linda Arline Hartung

As a lover of both music and beading challenges, I enjoy trying to incorporate beat, tempo, and rhythm into a piece of jewelry. When I saw these double-holed keystone components, I decided to create a crystal "polyrhythm" — the simultaneous sound of two or more independent rhythms. I changed the number and size of the crystals in each strand to create different tempos and expanded each strand to follow the curve of the neck. The challenge was creating three different patterns that would synchronize and finish at the precise measure. The result is a fabulous, undulating score of crystals that drapes beautifully in this necklace.

66I envisioned creating three strands, each with a distinct pattern, and then I connected them like bars of music using the keystone crystals.**99** –LAH

khaki
(simplicity)

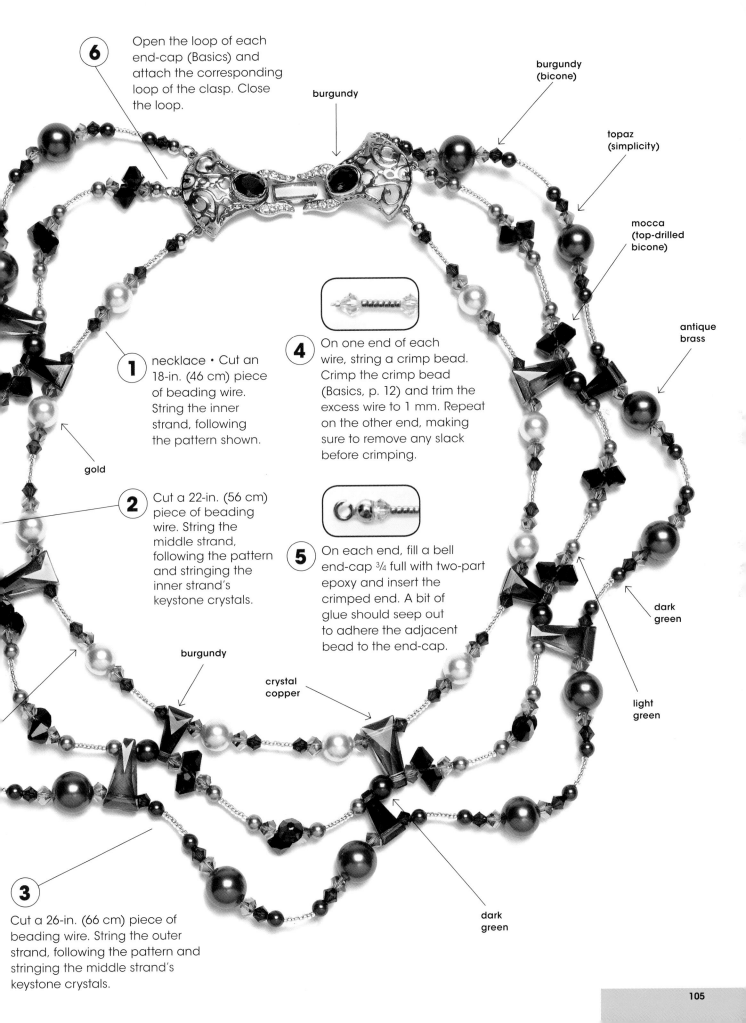

6 Open the loop of each end-cap (Basics) and attach the corresponding loop of the clasp. Close the loop.

burgundy

burgundy (bicone)

topaz (simplicity)

mocca (top-drilled bicone)

antique brass

1 necklace • Cut an 18-in. (46 cm) piece of beading wire. String the inner strand, following the pattern shown.

4 On one end of each wire, string a crimp bead. Crimp the crimp bead (Basics, p. 12) and trim the excess wire to 1 mm. Repeat on the other end, making sure to remove any slack before crimping.

gold

2 Cut a 22-in. (56 cm) piece of beading wire. String the middle strand, following the pattern and stringing the inner strand's keystone crystals.

5 On each end, fill a bell end-cap ¾ full with two-part epoxy and insert the crimped end. A bit of glue should seep out to adhere the adjacent bead to the end-cap.

dark green

light green

burgundy

crystal copper

3

Cut a 26-in. (66 cm) piece of beading wire. String the outer strand, following the pattern and stringing the middle strand's keystone crystals.

dark green

Supply notes

• In both versions of the necklace, the first two seed bead segments of the middle and outer strands are longer than the other segments. For instance, in the gold necklace, these "special" segments are 10 and 11 beads long respectively while all of the other segments are eight beads long. Adjust the number of beads for these special segments as necessary to create the desired curve of the strands.

• Even though 14° seed beads were used in both necklaces, there was a very slight difference in the size of the gold and silver beads. Where eight seed beads were used for the segments of the gold necklace, seven were used in the silver version. In larger quantities, the small size differences in the beads worked themselves out, so in the 10- and 11-bead special segments, no adjustments were made.
• Of the 57 4 mm pearls, 29 are in one color for the outer strand, and 28 are in a second color for the middle strand.
• Of the 77 4.5 mm simplicity crystals, 57 are in one color and 20 are in a second color. In the gold necklace, the second color is only used in the inner strand. In the silver necklace, the two colors are intermingled in the inner and outer strands.
• The flamenco clasp and fancy stone insets are sold separately. The stones should be set with two-part epoxy.

Supplies

necklace 16½ in. (41.9 cm)

- ◆ **6** 17 mm keystone crystals
- ◆ **6** 13 mm keystone crystals
- ◆ **14** 10 mm round pearls
- ◆ **10** 8 mm round pearls
- ◆ **6** 6 mm round pearls
- ◆ **57** 4 mm round pearls
- ◆ **28** 6 mm top-drilled bicone crystals
- ◆ **77** 4.5 mm simplicity crystals
- ◆ **51** 4 mm bicone or Xilion crystals
- ◆ 1 g 14° seed beads
- ◆ flexible beading wire, .018 or .019
- ◆ **6** crimp beads
- ◆ **6** bell end-caps
- ◆ three-strand flamenco clasp
- ◆ chainnose and roundnose pliers, or **2** pairs of chainnose pliers
- ◆ diagonal wire cutters
- ◆ crimping pliers (optional)
- ◆ two-part epoxy

earrings

- ◆ **2** 17 mm keystone crystals
- ◆ **2** 8 mm oval jump rings or 6 in. (15 cm) 18-gauge half-hard wire
- ◆ pair of earring wires with crystal insets
- ◆ chainnose and roundnose pliers, or **2** pairs of chainnose pliers
- ◆ diagonal wire cutters
- ◆ jump ring maker (optional)

Editor's note

The Xilion bead from Crystallized Swarovski Elements was introduced after Linda made the gold version of the necklace with bicones. We made the silver version with Xilions in place of the bicones to see if we would have to make any adjustments. No adjustments were necessary for the Xilions.

The top strand has 4 mm bicones. The bottom has 4 mm Xilions.

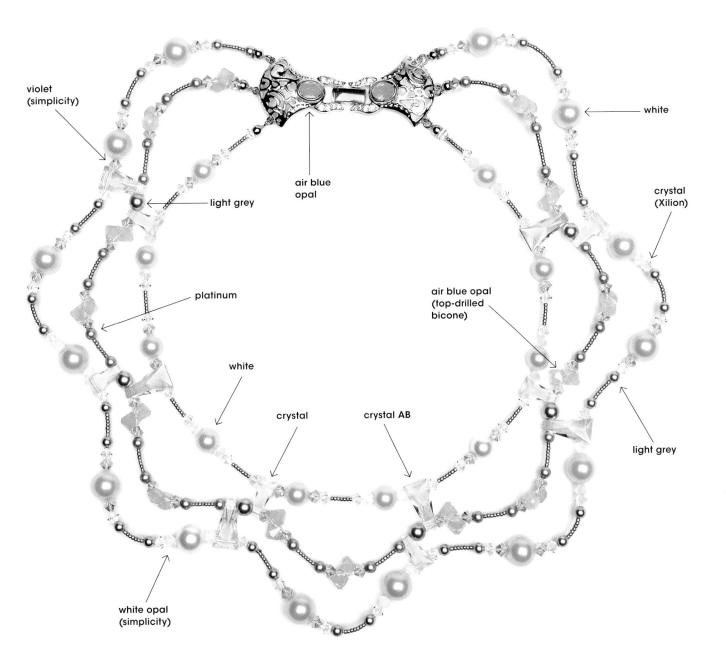

violet (simplicity)

white

air blue opal

light grey

crystal (Xilion)

platinum

air blue opal (top-drilled bicone)

white

crystal

crystal AB

light grey

white opal (simplicity)

1 earrings • Open an 8 mm oval jump ring (Basics), or make your own with a jump ring maker.

2 String a keystone crystal and close the jump ring.

3 Open the loop of an earring wire (Basics) and attach the dangle. Make a second earring.

Metal

& chain

Layers *of* links

Drape one long piece of chain in a modern bib necklace

Hands down, this will be the easiest bib necklace you ever make. Start with a few feet of pretty chain (I used brushed vermeil). Then, drape lengths back and forth across your hand and watch the bib take shape. If a few links hang askew, don't worry about it — go for a look that's sculptural, not symmetrical.

1 necklace • Open two oval jump rings (Basics, p. 12) and cut two 4–6-in. (10–15 cm) pieces of 7–10 mm link chain. Hold up your non-dominant hand and hang the end link of the 35–50 mm link chain on your thumb. Drape the chain and hang a link on your pinkie.

2 Continue draping the chain back and forth, hanging links on your thumb and pinkie, until the bib is the desired shape and size. (Simply redo the draping process if you don't like how the bib looks.) Do not trim the excess chain yet.

Supplies

necklace 16 in. (41 cm)
- 4–6 ft. (1.2–1.8 m) chain, 35–50 mm links
- 8–13 in. (20–33 cm) chain, 7–10 mm links
- **2** 6–12 mm oval jump rings
- **2** 4–6 mm jump rings
- toggle clasp
- chainnose and roundnose pliers, or **2** pairs of chainnose pliers
- diagonal wire cutters

earrings
- **2** 35–50 mm linked-circle findings
- **2** 5–6 mm jump rings (optional)
- pair of earring wires
- chainnose and roundnose pliers, or **2** pairs of chainnose pliers

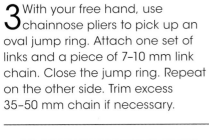

3 With your free hand, use chainnose pliers to pick up an oval jump ring. Attach one set of links and a piece of 7–10 mm link chain. Close the jump ring. Repeat on the other side. Trim excess 35–50 mm chain if necessary.

4 Check the fit, and trim 7–10 mm link chain from each end if necessary. On each end, use a 4–6 mm jump ring to attach half of a toggle clasp.

Tip

The larger the links, the less chain you'll need. I used 5 ft. (1.5 m) for my necklace.

earrings • Open the loop of an earring wire (Basics). Attach a linked-circle finding and close the loop. If the finding doesn't have a drilled hole, attach it with a jump ring (Basics). Make a second earring.

You can also use leftover small-link chain for earrings.

Triple-loop

Make these wirework earrings, 1–2–3

by Sonia Kumar

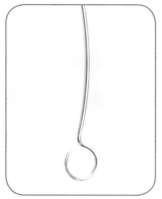

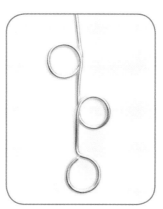

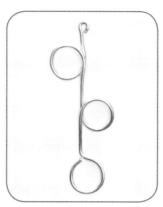

1 Cut a 6-in. (15 cm) piece of 16-gauge wire. Wrap one end around a cylindrical object to make a loop. Make a right-angle bend above the loop.

2 About ½ in. (1.3 cm) from the bend, form a second loop in the opposite direction. About ½ in. (1.3 cm) from the second loop, form a third loop in the same direction as the first.

3 About ½ in. (1.3 cm) from the third loop, use your roundnose pliers to form a small loop.

4 Cut a 3-in. (7.6 cm) piece of 28-gauge wire. Center a bead on the wire and place it in the bottom loop. Wrap each end around the loop. Repeat with the other loops.

Supplies

- **6** 8–10 mm round beads
- 12 in. (30 cm) 16-gauge dead-soft wire
- 18 in. (46 cm) 28-gauge half-hard wire
- pair of earring wires
- chainnose and roundnose pliers
- diagonal wire cutters
- cylindrical object, 8–10 mm diameter

❝I like that all of the supplies for these earrings can be bought at a craft store.❞ –SK

earrings

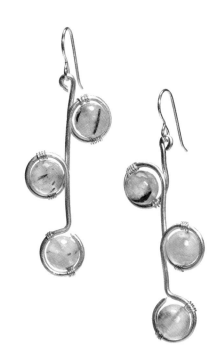

I needed a break from my typical complicated jewelry projects, so I pulled out a few beads and some wire and began to play. The result: easy, of-the-moment wire earrings.

5 Open the loop of an earring wire (Basics, p. 12) and attach the dangle. Close the loop. Make a second earring.

Design alternative

Make super-easy earrings with one loop at the bottom. Hammer the wire for sturdiness.

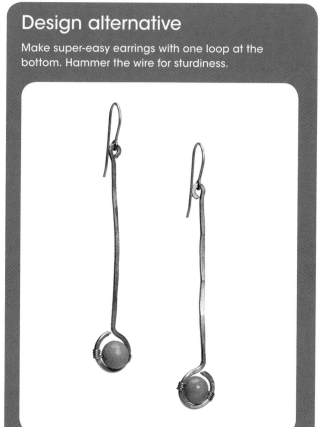

Copper wire and wood beads are inexpensive and widely available.

Climbing vine necklace

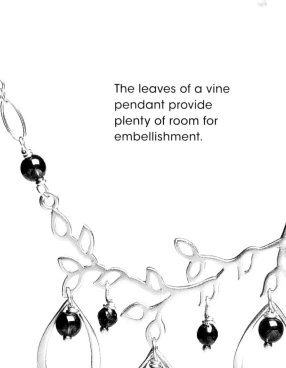

The leaves of a vine pendant provide plenty of room for embellishment.

Balance a pendant with leaf-shaped links

by Leah Rivers

For this necklace, I played with different sizes of marquise-shaped links until I found ones that looked proportional to the climbing vine pendant. The hammered links almost look like additional leaves hanging from the slender stem, and a few well-placed garnets look like ripened berries.

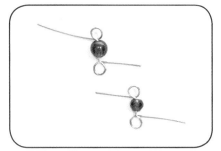

1 Cut a 2-in. (5 cm) piece of wire. Make the first half of a wrapped loop (Basics, p. 12). String a 4 mm bead and make the first half of a wrapped loop. Make two 4 mm bead connectors and two 3 mm bead connectors.

2 On a head pin, string a 4 mm bead and make the first half of a wrapped loop. Make three 4 mm bead units and two 3 mm bead units.

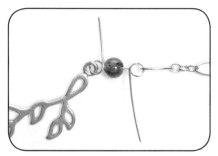

3 Decide how long you want your necklace to be, subtract 2 in. (5 cm), and cut a piece of chain to that length. Cut the chain in half. On each end loop of a vine pendant, attach a 4 mm connector and a chain. Complete the wraps.

Supplies

necklace 18 in. (46 cm)

- ◆ **5** 4 mm round beads
- ◆ **4** 3 mm faceted beads
- ◆ 8 in. (20 cm) 24-gauge half-hard wire
- ◆ 16–20 in. (41–51 cm) long-and-short-link chain, 3 mm links
- ◆ 47 mm climbing vine pendant
- ◆ 25 mm hammered marquise-shaped link
- ◆ **3** 20 mm hammered marquise-shaped links
- ◆ **5** 1½-in. (3.8 cm) decorative head pins
- ◆ hook-and-eye clasp
- ◆ chainnose and roundnose pliers
- ◆ diagonal wire cutters

Supplies from Nina Designs, ninadesigns.com.

66When I experience designer's block, I look back over designs I've made and continue to explore a particularly successful theme, technique, or color combination.99 —LR

Design alternative

For a bubbly silver version, use round links and slightly larger beads.

4 Attach a 25 mm marquise link, a 20 mm marquise link, a 4 mm bead unit and the bottom leaf of the vine pendant. Complete the wraps. On each side, attach a 20 mm link, a 4 mm bead unit, and a leaf of the pendant.

5 Attach each 3 mm bead unit to the vine pendant between marquise links.

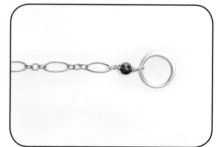

6 On each end, use a 3 mm connector to attach the chain and half of a hook-and-eye clasp.

Coiled-wire cuff

Ten steps to a cool cuff ◆ by **Sonia Kumar**

This bracelet is a challenge, but you can do it if you relax and take it one step at a time. Bend a long piece of 16-gauge wire to form a simple cuff frame, coil finer wire into two types of decorative shapes, then attach the shapes to the cuff using thinner wire. Along the way, you'll learn the basics of wire coiling and wrapping, and you'll end up with a beautiful bracelet.

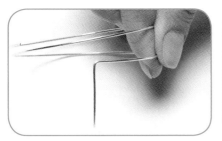

1 To make the frame: Cut a 15-in. (38 cm) piece of 16-gauge half-hard wire. Using nylon-jaw pliers, make a right-angle bend 1 in. (2.5 cm) from one end.

2 Make a right-angle bend 7 in. (18 cm) from the first bend. Make a right-angle bend 1 in. (2.5 cm) from the last bend.

3 On each wire end, make a loop. Open one loop (Basics, p. 12) and connect the ends. Close the loop. On a bench block or anvil, hammer the cuff.

4 To make an S coil: Cut a 4-in. (10 cm) piece of 16-gauge dead-soft wire. Wrap one end of the wire around the smallest part of your roundnose pliers. Make a successively larger spiral.

5 Repeat on the other end, turning the wire in the opposite direction. Use roundnose pliers to spread out each coil's center. Hammer the coils. Make six S coils.

6 To make a heart coil: Cut a 2-in. (5 cm) piece of 20-gauge wire. On each end, make a spiral as in step 4.

7 Center the wire around one jaw of your roundnose pliers, pulling the ends together to form a heart shape. Spread out each coil's center. Hammer the coils. Make 10 heart coils.

8 Wrap 24-gauge wire around one long side of the cuff three to six times. Attach the bottom of an S coil by wrapping the 24-gauge wire five to 10 times around the coil and the cuff. Wrap the 24-gauge around the cuff for about 1/2 in. (1.3 cm).

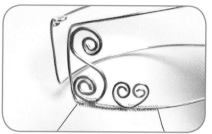

9 Attach a heart coil as in step 8. Wrap the 24-gauge wire around the cuff for about 1/2 in. (1.3 cm).

10 Continue wrapping and attaching S coils and heart coils. Wrap the other long side of the cuff with 24-gauge wire, attaching the top of each S coil as in step 8. Trim the 24-gauge wire and tuck the ends.

Design alternative

You can make a quick pair of coiled earrings without a huge time investment. Add a few beads for a flash of color.

Tips

- Often 16-gauge wire is sold rolled up. Don't straighten it. Use heavy-duty wire cutters to cut a two-coil length of wire from the roll.
- To make symmetrical coils, form two wire coils around your roundnose pliers at the same time.
- Be sure to use soft wire for the coils. Soft wire is easier to manipulate and your tools won't leave dings.

Supplies

- 15 in. (38 cm) 16-gauge half-hard wire
- 24 in. (61 cm) 16-gauge dead-soft wire or Artistic Wire
- 20 in. (51 cm) 20-gauge dead-soft wire or Artistic Wire
- 90 in. (2.3 m) 24-gauge half-hard wire
- nylon-jaw pliers
- roundnose pliers
- diagonal wire cutters
- bench block or anvil
- hammer

S·T·R·E·T·C·H
a short strand

A shortsighted purchase becomes a lesson in resourcefulness

by Jane Konkel

I didn't realize these rondelles were strung on a 7-in. (18 cm) strand until after I placed my order. Could I eke out a necklace, bracelet, and earrings with so few beads? Lesson learned: 11 big beads can go a long way when you include details like fancy chain and coiled-wire bead caps. There's nothing like an unexpected challenge to ignite creativity.

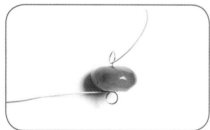

1 necklace • Cut a 6-in. (15 cm) piece of wire. About 2½ in. (6.4 cm) from one end, make the first half of a wrapped loop (Basics, p. 12). String a rondelle and make the first half of a wrapped loop perpendicular to the first.

2 Cut a 30-in. (76 cm) piece of chain. Attach a loop to each end of the chain and complete the wraps.

3 About 2 in. (5 cm) from the first rondelle, cut the chain and attach another rondelle unit. About 4 in. (10 cm) from the second rondelle, cut the chain and attach another rondelle unit.

1 bracelet • Cut an 8-in. (20 cm) piece of beading wire. String a spacer, an accent bead, a spacer, and a rondelle. String alternating spacers and rondelles until the beaded section is about 2½ in. (6.4 cm).

2 On one end, string a spacer, a crimp bead, a spacer, and a lobster claw clasp. Go back through the last few beads strung and tighten the wire.

3 On the other end of the beaded section, repeat step 2, substituting a 3–4-in. (7.6–10 cm) piece of chain for the clasp. On each end, crimp the crimp bead (Basics) and trim the excess wire. Close a crimp cover over each crimp.

66Necessity is
the mother of
invention.**99**
–Plato

1 earrings • On a head pin, string a spacer and a rondelle. Make the first half of a wrapped loop (Basics).

2 Cut a 1-in. (2.5 cm) piece of chain. Attach one end of the chain and the rondelle unit. Complete the wraps.

3 Open the loop of an earring wire (Basics). Attach the dangle and close the loop. Make a second earring.

Supply note

These large chalcedony rondelles range in color and size. Choose two similar beads for earrings before you cut the strand.

Tip

Make the most of your wire by using it as a design element. When making wrapped loops, continue the wraps by coiling the wire over the bead.

Supplies

necklace 34 in. (86 cm)

- 7-in. (18 cm) strand 17–24 mm rondelles
- 18 in. (46 cm) 22-gauge half-hard wire
- 28–32 in. (71–81 cm) three-ring design chain, 6–12 mm links
- chainnose and roundnose pliers
- diagonal wire cutters

bracelet

- 18–24 mm accent bead
- **5–7** 17–24 mm rondelles left over from necklace
- **8–12** 4 mm spacers
- flexible beading wire, .018 or .019
- **2** crimp beads
- **2** crimp covers
- lobster claw clasp
- 3–4 in. (7.6–10 cm) three-ring design chain, 6–12 mm links
- chainnose or crimping pliers
- diagonal wire cutters

earrings

- **2** 17–24 mm rondelles left over from necklace
- **2** 4 mm spacers
- 2 in. (5 cm) three-ring design chain, 6–12 mm links
- **2** 1½-in. (3.8 cm) head pins
- pair of earring wires
- chainnose and roundnose pliers
- diagonal wire cutters

Figure-8 earrings

Create pretty earrings with two turns of your roundnose pliers

by Catherine Hodge

Supplies

- **2** 7–10 mm briolettes
- 3 in. (7.6 cm) 20- or 22-gauge half-hard wire
- 10 in. (25 cm) 24- or 26-gauge half-hard wire
- pair of earring posts with ear nuts
- chainnose and roundnose pliers
- diagonal wire cutters
- bench block or anvil
- hammer

This basic shape offers infinite opportunities for experimentation: Make loops round or drop-shaped, make one loop larger than the other, or attach the larger loop to the earring post. You can also vary how you incorporate the figure 8s: Use heavy wire to make a connector or the eye half of a hook-and-eye clasp.

Tip

To save wire, don't cut a piece before making the figure 8. Instead, leave the wire on the roll. Trim only after you've made the second loop.

1 Cut a 1½-in. (3.8 cm) piece of 20- or 22-gauge wire. Using roundnose pliers, roll one end of the wire to make a loop.

2 Around a larger part of your roundnose pliers, roll the other end of the wire in the opposite direction to make a loop. Trim the excess wire.

3 On a bench block or anvil, gently hammer the front and back of the figure 8.

4 Cut a 5-in. (13 cm) piece of 24- or 26-gauge wire. String a briolette and make a set of wraps above it (Basics, p. 12). Make the first half of a wrapped loop (Basics) perpendicular to the briolette.

5 Attach the briolette unit and one loop of the figure 8. Complete the wraps, continuing until the wraps touch the top of the briolette.

6 Open the loop of an earring post (Basics). Attach the dangle and close the loop. Make a second earring.

Suspended **silver**

Lightweight wire circles make a great pendant

by Dawn Davis

To make the pendant on my necklace, I used three dowels with different diameters, but you can experiment with other cylindrical objects to make these easy components.

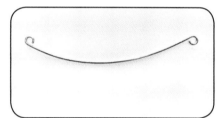

1 necklace • To make a 10 mm (small) circle component, cut a 3-in. (7.6 cm) piece of wire. Make a loop on each end in opposite directions.

2 Position one loop on the third smallest tier of a mandrel or on a ³⁄₈-in. (1 cm) dowel, and pull the wire around one full rotation.

3 Make a right-angle bend with the first loop. Pull the wire around the stem.

4 Place the tip of your roundnose pliers in the loop and coil the wire. Center the coil in the circle.

Tips

• Depending on the orientation of your earring wire's loop, you may need to turn the circle's loop before attaching. Use chainnose pliers to grasp and twist the loop until it's perpendicular.
• You can texturize the circles with the ball end of a chasing hammer.

Supplies

necklace 16 in. (41 cm)
◆ 11½ in. (29.2 cm) 18- or 20-gauge wire
◆ 16-in. (41 cm) finished snake chain
◆ chainnose and roundnose pliers
◆ diagonal wire cutters
◆ Fiskars Right Angle mandrel or **3** dowels: ³⁄₈ in. (1 cm), ½ in. (1.3 cm), and ¾ in. (1.9 cm)

earrings
◆ 13 in. (33 cm) 18- or 20-gauge wire
◆ pair of earring wires
◆ chainnose and roundnose pliers
◆ diagonal wire cutters
◆ Fiskars Right Angle mandrel or **3** dowels: ³⁄₈ in. (1 cm), ½ in. (1.3 cm), and ¾ in. (1.9 cm)

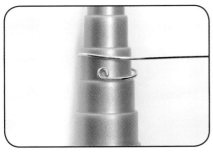

5 Make a 13 mm (medium) circle component with a 3½-in. (8.9 cm) piece of wire on the fifth tier of the mandrel or on a ½-in. (1.3 cm) dowel.

6 Make a 19 mm (large) circle component with a 5-in. (13 cm) piece of wire on the eighth tier of the mandrel or on a ¾-in. (1.9 cm) dowel.

7 Open the loop (Basics, p. 12) of the small circle component. Attach the medium component and close the loop.

8 Attach the medium component to the large, and the large component to the chain.

1 earrings • Follow necklace steps 1 through 5 to make a small and a medium circle component.

2 Attach the components as in necklace step 7.

3 Open the loop of an earring wire (Basics) and attach the dangle. Close the loop. Make a second earring.

Wire-wrapped hoops

Exotic-looking earrings stand on their own

by Felicia Cantillo

Form hoops with 18-gauge wire, then make tidy wraps of 26-gauge wire around them. Even if you've never wrapped wire before, you'll master it quickly with this project. I used round faceted garnet beads as accents, but you can easily substitute round crystals.

Supplies

- **4** 9–10 mm faceted oval beads
- **38–42** 3 mm faceted round beads
- **20** 3 mm round spacers
- **20** 3 mm flat spacers
- 9 in. (23 cm) 18-gauge wire
- 80 in. (2 m) 26-gauge wire
- 3 in. (7.6 cm) chain, 3–4 mm links
- **12** 1½-in. (3.8 cm) head pins
- pair of earring wires
- chainnose and roundnose pliers
- nylon-jaw pliers (optional)
- diagonal wire cutters
- 1-in. (2.5 cm) diameter cylindrical object

1 On a head pin, string: round spacer, flat spacer, round bead, flat spacer, round spacer. Make a wrapped loop (Basics, p. 12). Make a second round-bead unit. On a head pin, string: round spacer, flat spacer, oval bead, flat spacer, round spacer. Make a wrapped loop. Set these bead units aside for step 5.

2 Make a round-bead unit and an oval-bead unit as in step 1 but do not complete the wraps. Cut a four-link and a five-link piece of chain. Attach the round-bead unit to the four-link chain and complete the wraps. Attach the oval-bead unit to the five-link chain and complete the wraps. Set the dangles aside for step 7.

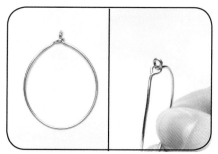

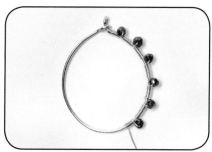

3 To make the earring frame: Cut a 4½-in. (11.4 cm) piece of 18-gauge wire. Wrap the wire around a cylindrical object so the ends cross. On each end, make a plain loop (Basics). Bend one loop so it is perpendicular to the other. Open the other loop (Basics), attach the wire to the stem, and close the loop.

4 Cut a 40-in. (1 m) piece of 26-gauge wire. At the top of the frame near a loop, wrap one end of the wire eight to 10 times. String a round bead, and make eight to 10 more wraps. Continue making wraps and stringing beads until just above the bottom of the frame. Make two to five wraps.

5 String a round-bead unit from step 1 and make five to eight wraps. String the oval-bead unit from step 1 and make five to eight wraps. String the remaining round-bead unit and make two to five wraps.

6 Continue making wraps and stringing beads as in step 4 until you reach the other loop of the frame. Trim the excess wire and tuck the end.

7 Open the frame's perpendicular loop and attach the dangles from step 2. Close the loop.

8 Trim the head from a head pin and make the first half of a wrapped loop. String a round bead and make the first half of a wrapped loop. Attach one loop to the frame and the other loop to an earring wire and complete the wraps. Make a second earring.

Tip

If 40 in. (1 m) of 26-gauge wire is too much for you to handle when wrapping, cut the wire in half and wrap with one 20-in. (51 cm) piece. When the wire gets short, end it as in step 6. Begin wrapping the next 20-in. piece where you left off.

A filigree pendant adds
another layer of interest
to crystals, glass, and chain

by Denise Yezbak Moore

Winged style

This bracelet was inspired by Czechoslovakian costume jewelry from the 1920s and '30s. Blending the brass and colored glass with the dragonfly gives the piece a bohemian flare that transcends fads, and the colors go well with the changing seasons. Use a Venetian coin bead in gold, green, and burnt orange for an autumnal look or a lapis-colored bead for the winter months ahead.

1 bracelet • Place the pendant in the desired position on the Venetian bead and mark where you'll bend the wings and tail with a crayon or grease pencil.

2 Using roundnose pliers, bend the pendant to fit the bead. Position the pendant against the bead before making any final adjustments. Glue the pendant to the bead if desired (Tip, p. 128).

3 Cut a 4-in. (10 cm) piece of wire. Make a wrapped loop (Basics, p. 12). String a bicone crystal, the pendant unit, and a bicone. Make a wrapped loop.

Design alternative

Switch from air to water by substituting a dolphin (far left) for the dragonfly and using brighter, aquatic colors for the crystals. Save yourself some loop wrapping without losing any sparkle by attaching the crystals directly to the chain.

4 Cut a 2½-in. (6.4 cm) piece of wire. Make a wrapped loop. String a bicone, a 10 mm round crystal, and a bicone. Make a wrapped loop. Make four 10 mm units. Make two more, substituting an 8 mm round crystal for the 10 mm.

On a head pin, string a bicone, a 10 mm round, and a bicone. Make a wrapped loop.

On a head pin, string a bicone and an 8 mm round. Make a wrapped loop.

5 Open a 4 mm jump ring (Basics). Attach two 10 mm units. Close the jump ring. Use another jump ring to attach an 8 mm double-bicone unit on one end. Repeat to make a second beaded strand.

6 Cut two 3½-in. (8.9 cm) pieces of chain. Open one chain's end link and attach one end of the beaded strand and the 10 mm head pin unit. Close the link. Repeat with the second piece of chain, substituting a clasp for the head pin unit.

7 Use a jump ring to attach the remaining end of a beaded strand and a chain to each wrapped loop of the pendant unit.
String the 8 mm head pin unit over the dragonfly's tail.

1 earrings • Cut three links of chain. On a head pin, string a 10 mm round crystal, a bead cap, a Venetian bead, and an end link of the chain. Make a wrapped loop (Basics).

2 Open a 4 mm jump ring (Basics). Attach a dragonfly charm to the chain and close the jump ring. Open the loop of an earring wire (Basics) and attach the dangle. Close the loop. Make a second earring to match the first.

❝I am a freestyle designer — I do not pre-plan any of the pieces I design. The materials I am using at the time inspire me.❞ —DYM

Supplies

bracelet
- 47 mm dragonfly pendant
- 30 mm Venetian coin bead
- **5** 10 mm round crystals
- **3** 8 mm round crystals
- **17** 4–5 mm bicone crystals
- 19 in. (48 cm) 22-gauge half-hard wire
- 7 in. (18 cm) cable chain, 10 mm links
- **2** 2-in. (5 cm) head pins
- roundnose pliers
- diagonal wire cutters
- crayon or grease pencil
- jewelry glue (optional)

earrings
- **2** 20 mm Venetian coin beads
- **2** 17 mm dragonfly charms
- **2** 10 mm round crystals
- **2** 10 mm bead caps
- ½ in. (1.3 cm) cable chain, 3 mm links
- **2** 2-in. (5 cm) head pins
- **2** 4 mm jump rings
- pair of earring wires
- chainnose and roundnose pliers
- diagonal wire cutters

Tip

Add a dab of glue to the back of the dragonfly pendant for extra security before wrapping it around the bead.

Floral wreath
earrings

Dangle flower beads from copper rings ◆ by Lori Anderson

Flowers like the chrysanthemum that bloom in the fall bring a bit of summer into the cooler autumn months. Carry that transitional beauty into your jewelry creations, and make multiple versions with various glass flower beads for a bouquet of options.

1 On a head pin, string a round bead and a flower bead. Using the largest part of your roundnose pliers, make the first half of a wrapped loop (Basics, p. 12). Make three flower units.

2 Attach a flower unit to a copper ring and complete the wraps. Attach two more flower units.

Supplies

- **2** 1–1½-in. (2.5–3.8 cm) copper rings
- **6** 8–10 mm flower beads
- **6** 3–4 mm round beads
- **6** 2-in. (5 cm) head pins
- **2** 6 mm jump rings
- pair of earring wires
- chainnose and roundnose pliers
- diagonal wire cutters

3 Open a jump ring (Basics). Attach the ring and the loop of an earring wire. Close the jump ring. Make a second earring.

Design alternative

Use round beads instead of flowers to make a simpler statement.

Fan earr

Chain earrings are gorgeous and gratifying

by Jessica Tiemens

I get such satisfaction from making earrings: They're quick and easy, and I'm almost always delighted with the results. Small crystals strung on wire anchor the chains, giving the earrings just enough heft to hang elegantly.

1 Cut a 2½-in. (6.4 cm) piece of wire. Make a wrapped loop (Basics, p. 12). String a rondelle and make the first half of a wrapped loop perpendicular to the first loop.

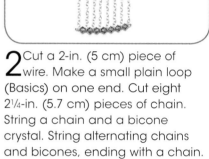

2 Cut a 2-in. (5 cm) piece of wire. Make a small plain loop (Basics) on one end. Cut eight 2¼-in. (5.7 cm) pieces of chain. String a chain and a bicone crystal. String alternating chains and bicones, ending with a chain. Make a plain loop.

3 Attach the other ends of the chains to the unwrapped loop of the rondelle unit. Complete the wraps.

4 Open a jump ring (Basics) and attach the dangle and the loop of an earring wire. Close the jump ring. Make a second earring.

ings

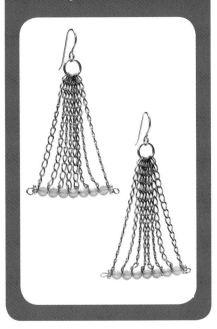

Tip

I used jump rings so that my earrings would have a lot of movement, but you can omit the jump ring in step 4. Instead, make the loops parallel on the rondelle unit, then attach the loop of an earring wire.

Supplies

- ◆ **2** 6 mm crystal rondelles
- ◆ **14** 4 mm bicone crystals
- ◆ 38 in. (97 cm) chain, 1–2 mm links
- ◆ 9 in. (23 cm) 24-gauge half-hard wire
- ◆ **2** 4 mm jump rings
- ◆ pair of earring wires
- ◆ chainnose and roundnose pliers
- ◆ diagonal wire cutters

66Necessity inspired these earrings. I wanted to use two crystal rondelles I bought on impulse, and I happened to have smaller crystals and chain.**99** – JT

Brass
leaves

Make quick
jewelry with
antiqued brass
leaves and
findings

by Kellie Sutton

Etched brass components combine with pearls in shades of gold and green to express the season's muted tones. The knotted toggle bar — reminiscent of a twig — slips through a hammered ring for a pretty clasp.

1 necklace • On a head pin, string a pearl. Make a wrapped loop (Basics, p. 12). Make five pearl units, stringing a bead cap on one of them.

2 Open a 9–10 mm oval link (Basics). Attach a leaf charm and the largest pearl unit. Close the link.

3 Use a 9–10 mm round link to attach a pearl unit, the oval link, and a pearl unit.

4 Use a round link to attach two pearl units, the first round link, and a hammered ring.

5 Decide how long you want your necklace to be and cut a piece of chain to that length. Use a 4–5 mm jump ring to attach one end and the hole of the hammered ring.

6 Check the fit, and trim chain if necessary. Use one or two jump rings to attach a toggle bar.

Tips

• If your brass head pins do not go through the pearls, use 24- or 26-gauge gold-filled head pins instead.
• If necessary, use a bead reamer to enlarge the holes of the charms.

1 earrings • On a head pin, string a pearl. Make a wrapped loop (Basics). Make three pearl units, stringing a bead cap on one of them.

2 Open a 9–10 mm oval link (Basics). Attach a leaf charm and the smallest pearl unit. Close the link.

3 Use a 9–10 mm round link to attach a pearl unit, the oval link, a pearl unit, and the loop of an earring wire. Make a second earring the mirror image of the first.

Design alternative

For vintage variety, make a bracelet with chunky chain, pearls, and crystals. I used faux pearls, which have larger holes that can accommodate antique brass head pins.

Supplies

necklace 18½ in. (47 cm)
- ◆ 38 mm woodland leaf charm
- ◆ 22 mm hammered ring, with drilled hole
- ◆ 5 4–10 mm pearls
- ◆ 8 mm foliage bead cap
- ◆ 2 9–10 mm round links
- ◆ 9–10 mm oval link
- ◆ 16–20 in. (41–51 cm) chain, 3–4 mm links
- ◆ 5 1½-in. (3.8 cm) head pins
- ◆ 2–3 4–5 mm jump rings
- ◆ love knot toggle bar
- ◆ chainnose and roundnose pliers
- ◆ diagonal wire cutters

earrings
- ◆ 2 18 mm woodland leaf charms
- ◆ 6 4–10 mm pearls, 2 of each size and color
- ◆ 2 8 mm foliage bead caps
- ◆ 2 9–10 mm round links
- ◆ 2 9–10 mm oval links
- ◆ 6 1½-in. (3.8 cm) head pins
- ◆ pair of earring wires
- ◆ chainnose and roundnose pliers
- ◆ diagonal wire cutters

Note: For the 9–10 mm links, use either jump rings or individual links of chain.

Raising the bar

Make a bracelet with an unexpected use of spacer bars
◆ by Jessica Tiemens

Spacer bars are normally used to align multiple strands of beads, but why relegate them to a special occasion on a multistrand necklace? Here, the bars play a major role in a bracelet you can wear everyday. Let your bars shine!

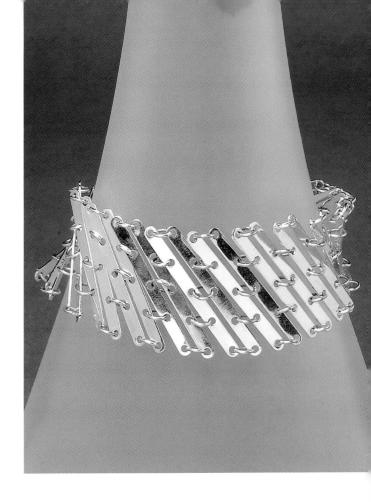

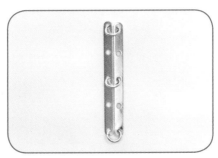

1 Open a jump ring (Basics, p. 12). Attach the first holes of two spacer bars. Close the jump ring. Use jump rings to attach the third and fifth holes.

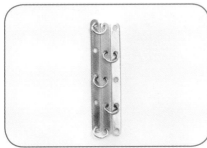

2 Use jump rings to attach the second and fourth holes of the second spacer bar and a third spacer bar.

Supplies

- **28–32** spacer bars with five holes
- **70–80** 5 mm jump rings
- **2** 4 mm oval jump rings
- toggle clasp
- **2** pairs of pliers (choose from chainnose, roundnose, or bentnose)

3 Continue using jump rings to attach spacer bars as in steps 1 and 2 until your bracelet is within 2 in. (5 cm) of the finished length.

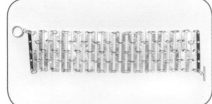

4 Use an oval jump ring to attach half of a toggle clasp to the first hole of a spacer bar on one end. On the other end, use an oval jump ring to attach the other half of the clasp and the fifth hole of a spacer bar.

Scrapbooking
embellishments
make unexpected
beading
components

by Monica Han

Say it with
style

I found a package of copper embellishments in the sticker section at a craft store. They're meant for scrapbooks and greeting cards, but I thought they'd make great jewelry components. The results? The bracelet and earrings say it all. When I went back to get more, I discovered that scrapbooking materials don't stay around too long. Luckily, I found other embellishments that, with a few adjustments, worked just as well.

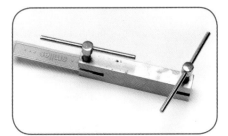

1 bracelet • Use a hole punch to add holes to scrapbook embellishments if necessary. Each embellishment should have a hole on each end.

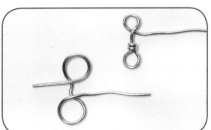

2 Cut a 2-in. (5 cm) piece of 24-gauge wire. Using the largest part of your roundnose pliers, make the first half of a wrapped loop (Basics, p. 12) on each end. Repeat. Make a third unit with smaller loops and complete the wraps on one end.

3 Attach the embellishments with the large-loop units. Complete the wraps as you go. On one end, attach the small-loop unit. Complete the wraps.

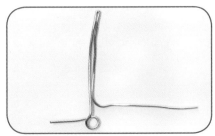

4 Cut a 5-in. (13 cm) piece of 20-gauge wire. Fold the wire in half. On one end, about 1 in. (2.5 cm) from the fold, make a right-angle bend. On the other end, make the first half of a wrapped loop.

5 Wrap the angled end around the stem and trim the excess wire. Using roundnose pliers, bend the folded section of the wire into a hook.

6 Attach the hook's loop to the hole of an embellishment. Complete the wraps.

7 Cut a 2-in. (5 cm) piece of 24-gauge wire. Make a plain loop (Basics) on one end. String a spacer, three disks, and a spacer. Make the first half of a wrapped loop. Make 16 bead units.

8 Attach eight bead units to each large-loop unit as shown. Complete the wraps.

Supplies

bracelet

- ◆ **3** 2-in. (5 cm) scrapbook embellishments
- ◆ **48** 4 mm disk beads
- ◆ **32** 2 mm round spacers
- ◆ 5 in. (13 cm) 20-gauge half-hard wire
- ◆ 38 in. (97 cm) 24-gauge half-hard wire
- ◆ chainnose and roundnose pliers
- ◆ diagonal wire cutters
- ◆ hole punch (optional)

earrings

- ◆ **2** 1-in. (2.5 cm) scrapbook embellishments
- ◆ **18** 4 mm disk beads
- ◆ **12** 2 mm round spacers
- ◆ 12 in. (30 cm) 24-gauge half-hard wire
- ◆ **2** 6 mm jump rings
- ◆ pair of earring wires
- ◆ chainnose and roundnose pliers
- ◆ diagonal wire cutters
- ◆ hole punch (optional)

1 earrings • Use a hole punch to add holes to scrapbook embellishments if necessary. Following bracelet step 7, make three bead units. Attach them to one end of the embellishment and complete the wraps.

2 Open a jump ring (Basics). Attach the dangle and the loop of an earring wire. Close the jump ring. Make a second earring.

Design alternative

Use knotted leather cord and beads to make an earthier version of the bracelet or silk cord for a softer look.

Tips

• Don't worry if you can't find the exact embellishments used here. There is a range of options in both the jewelry and scrapbooking aisles.

• Before stringing, remove the backing from the adhesive on the embellishments. Soak them in soapy water or use nail polish remover or Goo Gone to remove the adhesive.
• If you are making holes in the embellishments, mark the spot first with a pen for accuracy.
• In the copper version of the bracelet, I used 20-gauge wire and 4 mm rectangular beads instead of disks. The styles of the bead units are varied, with coils on the ends of some instead of loops.

Layered
leaves

Create a pair of cascading earrings with mixed-metal charms ◆ **by Candie Cooper**

Metallic tones with a clear crystal will pair well with most color palettes.

When I saw these lightweight leaves, I knew they would be perfect for earrings. Their slender profile dangled from chain creates a beautiful trickle-down effect with lots of movement and texture. The leaves come in silver, gold, and copper finishes — use all three for subtle contrast and realistic variation.

1 On a decorative head pin, string a crystal and a spacer. Make a wrapped loop (Basics, p. 12).

2 Cut a 10-link piece of chain. Open a jump ring (Basics) and attach the crystal unit and the bottom link. Close the jump ring. Use a jump ring to attach an earring wire and the top link.

Supplies

- ◆ **20** 8–9 mm leaf charms in three finishes
- ◆ **2** 8 mm round crystals
- ◆ **2** 3–4 mm flat spacers
- ◆ 4 in. (10 cm) chain, 3–4 mm links
- ◆ **2** 1½-in. (3.8 cm) decorative head pins
- ◆ **24** 3–4 mm jump rings
- ◆ pair of earring wires
- ◆ chainnose and roundnose pliers
- ◆ diagonal wire cutters

3 Use jump rings to attach a leaf to each link. Make a second earring.

HOOP dee-do

Tiny wire wraps take hoop earrings to the next level

by Ann Westby

Wire wrapping is my first love, and what better way to attach an earring wire and briolette than to wire-wrap some loops? The wire wrapping lends another texture to the design, and I get to make my own findings.

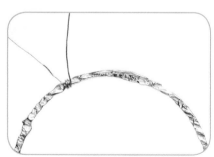

1 Cut a 16-in. (41 cm) piece of wire. Leaving a 2-in. (5 cm) tail, wrap the wire snugly around a hoop.

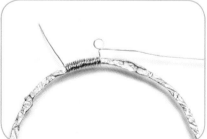

2 Continue wrapping the wire, covering about ¼ in. (6 mm) of the hoop. Make a wrapped loop (Basics, p. 12) but don't trim the excess wire.

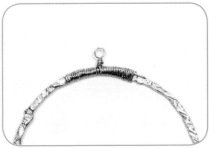

3 Continue wrapping the wire around ¼ in. (6 mm) of the hoop. Trim the excess wire and tuck the ends with chainnose pliers.

4 Repeat steps 1 to 3 on the opposite side of the hoop.

5 Cut a 6-in. (15 cm) piece of wire. String a briolette and make a set of wraps above it (Basics). Make the first half of a wrapped loop perpendicular to the briolette.

6 Attach the briolette unit to one of the loops of the hoop. Complete the wraps, covering part of the briolette if desired.

7 Open the loop of an earring wire (Basics). Attach the hoop and close the loop. Make a second earring.

Supplies

- **2** 9–13 mm briolettes or teardrop-shaped beads, top drilled
- **2** 40–50 mm metal hoops
- 76 in. (1.9 m) 28-gauge wire
- pair of earring wires
- chainnose and roundnose pliers
- diagonal wire cutters

Tips

• Choose delicate (and not overly large) briolettes that won't overwhelm the tiny wire wraps.
• For a more affordable pair of earrings, use craft wire instead of sterling or gold-filled.
• It's handy to have a 2-in. (5 cm) tail when you begin the wraps. The extra wire will allow you to make additional wraps if you need to even out the sides.
• If you use handmade hoops, you might find slight variations in size or shape.

"I never measure. I cut a piece of wire a little shorter than the length of my arm. I work with that wire until I run out and then cut another one." —AW

Coiled bead

Make wire coils to cap glass beads or pearls, and add spacers and metal accent beads to match

by Susan White

Bead caps are a bead's favorite accessory — and when your beads are beautifully adorned, so are you! Faceted gemstones and crystals keep the look from being too heavy metal.

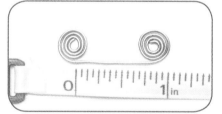

1 Cut a 5½-in. (14 cm) piece of wire. Using roundnose pliers, make a loop at one end. Grasp the loop with chainnose or flatnose pliers and press the next ⅛ in. (3 mm) of the wire tail against the loop. Reposition the pliers and repeat, making an 8–9 mm coil.

2 Repeat step 1 on the other end, leaving ¾ in. (1.9 cm) of straight wire between the coils.

Supplies

- ◆ **3–4** 11–15 mm glass beads or pearls
- ◆ **2–8** 6–11 mm metal accent beads
- ◆ **3–11** 4–8 mm gemstone or crystal accent beads
- ◆ **4–12** 6 mm spacers
- ◆ **2** 3 mm spacers
- ◆ **6–10** bead caps
- ◆ flexible beading wire, .014 or .015
- ◆ 17–22 in. (43–56 cm) 20-gauge dead-soft wire
- ◆ **2** crimp beads
- ◆ **2** crimp covers
- ◆ toggle clasp
- ◆ chainnose or flatnose pliers
- ◆ roundnose pliers
- ◆ diagonal wire cutters
- ◆ crimping pliers (optional)

caps

3 Twist one coil upside down, forming an S shape. Use roundnose pliers to gently push out the center of each coil.

4 Place one coil over a hole of an 11–15 mm bead. Gently pull the other coil over the other hole of the bead so that the wire loosely wraps around the bead. Adjust the coils as necessary (see Tip).

Tip

In step 4, temporarily string the bead and coils on a head pin or piece of scrap wire. Using chainnose or flatnose pliers, loosen or tighten the coils to hold the bead snugly and to align the center of the coils with the bead's holes.

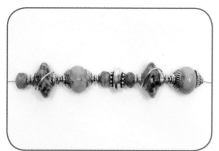

5 Repeat steps 1 through 4 to make three or four wire-capped beads. Cut a piece of beading wire (Basics, p. 12). String wire-capped beads, accent beads, spacers, and bead caps as desired.

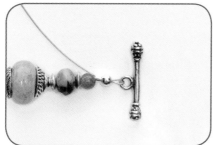

6 On each end, attach half of a toggle clasp (Basics). Close a crimp cover over each crimp.

Brise Soleil necklace

Bend and assemble wire in homage to an architectural wonder

by Brenda Schweder

Milwaukee, Wis., is home to amazing architecture, so it's no surprise to those of us who live here that artist, architect, and engineer Santiago Calatrava chose to erect one of his masterpieces where Lake Michigan meets our humble city. The *Burke Brise Soleil* — a moveable, wing-like sunscreen that rests on top of the Milwaukee Art Museum — is genius. Watching its wings open and close above the museum's vaulted glass ceiling takes my breath away. This magnificent sculpture inspired my architectural jewelry.

Supplies

necklace 20 in. (51 cm)
- 87–91 in. (2.2–2.3 m) 16-gauge dead-soft steel wire
- flexible beading wire, .018 or .019
- flatnose and round-nose pliers
- heavy-duty wire cutters
- bench block and utility hammer
- G-S Hypo Cement
- large cylindrical object
- Liquid Paper for marking wire
- metal file
- microcrystalline wax and soft rag
- painter's tape for marking pliers
- steel-wire brush

Tip

Working with rebar tie wire requires hand strength. Conserve yours by practicing with craft wire first.

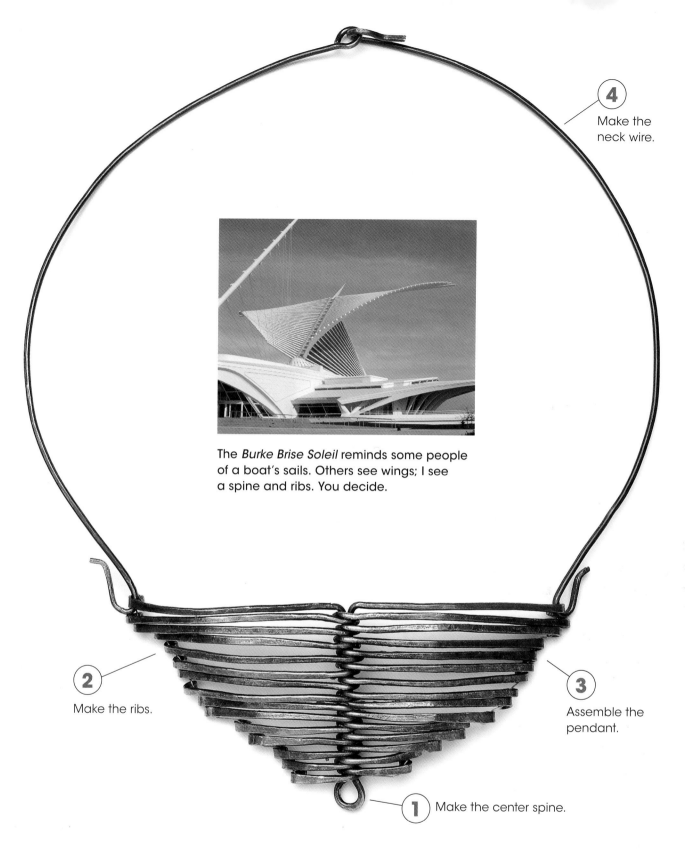

4 Make the neck wire.

The *Burke Brise Soleil* reminds some people of a boat's sails. Others see wings; I see a spine and ribs. You decide.

2 Make the ribs.

3 Assemble the pendant.

1 Make the center spine.

1 To make the spine:
a Cut a 24-in. (61 cm) piece of wire. Mark the center with Liquid Paper. Position the largest part of your roundnose pliers on the mark and pull the ends around your pliers. With flatnose pliers, squeeze the ends together to form a loop.

b Hammer both sides of the wire.

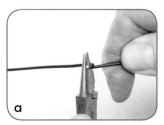

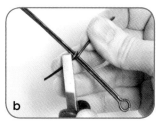

2 To make the ribs:
Cut a 2-in. (5 cm) piece of wire. Cut 13 more pieces, each ¼ in. (6 mm) longer than the last. The last rib should be 5¼ in. (13.3 cm) long.

Straighten each rib wire and mark the center point on each.

a Position your roundnose pliers over the mark. Pull each end of the rib completely around the pliers.

b Check that the center loop fits snugly on the spine. Adjust the loop if necessary and mark the jaws of your roundnose pliers with tape so you make the same size loop on each rib. Repeat with each rib.

c Hammer each side of each rib, flattening them to 1 mm. Hammer each tip perpendicular to the loop, flattening them to less than 1 mm. File the ends.

d Make a small loop at the tips of each rib. Form a slight curve on each side.

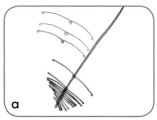

Supply note

Rebar tie wire is a low-carbon, black, annealed-steel wire. You can find it in the concrete and fencing supplies department at your local hardware or home-improvement store.

3 To assemble the pendant:

a Lay out the ribs from shortest to longest. String the shortest rib on the spine first. Repeat with the remaining ribs.

b Bend the spine ends in opposite directions to make the top rib. Trim the ends and make a loop on each end.

c Cut a 24-in. (61 cm) piece of beading wire. Center the loop of the spine. On each side, string each rib's loop. Adjust the ribs. Tie a surgeon's knot around the top rib's loop, sliding the knot toward the back of the pendant. Apply glue to the knot and trim the wire tails.

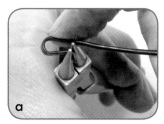

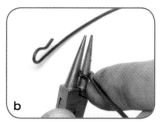

4 To make the neck wire:
a Cut two 6–8-in. (15–20 cm) pieces of wire. Hammer one end of each wire and file the end. Make a hook.

b On the remaining end of one wire, make a large plain loop (Basics, p. 12). Hammer the loop. On the remaining end of the other wire, make a second hook.

c Insert a hook into each top loop of the pendant. Pull the ends of each piece around a large cylindrical object, like a necklace form covered with a plastic bag.

d Clean with a brush. Apply wax with a soft rag. Allow to dry.

Wire-wonder earrings

Add crystals and spacers to complement intricate wire beads

by Christianne Camera

Sometimes you come across a bead that is so wonderful you just need to get out of its way while it becomes a beautiful piece of jewelry. The key is keeping it simple.

Supplies

- **2** 16 mm round wire beads
- **2** 8 mm round crystals
- **4** 4 mm bicone or round crystals
- **2** 4 mm flat spacers
- 4 in. (10 cm) 22-gauge half-hard wire
- **2** 2-in. (5 cm) head pins
- pair of earring wires
- chainnose and roundnose pliers
- diagonal wire cutters

1 Cut a 2-in. (5 cm) piece of wire. Make a plain loop (Basics, p. 12). String an 8 mm crystal, a spacer, and a 4 mm crystal. Make a plain loop.

2 On a head pin, string a wire bead and a 4 mm crystal. Make a plain loop.

3 Open each loop of the crystal unit (Basics). Attach the wire-bead unit and close the loop. Attach the dangle and an earring wire and close the loop. Make a second earring.

Tip

Never be afraid to break the rules (even your own). Even though the wire beads look great in a simple earring, pairing them with another interesting component can create a real showstopper.

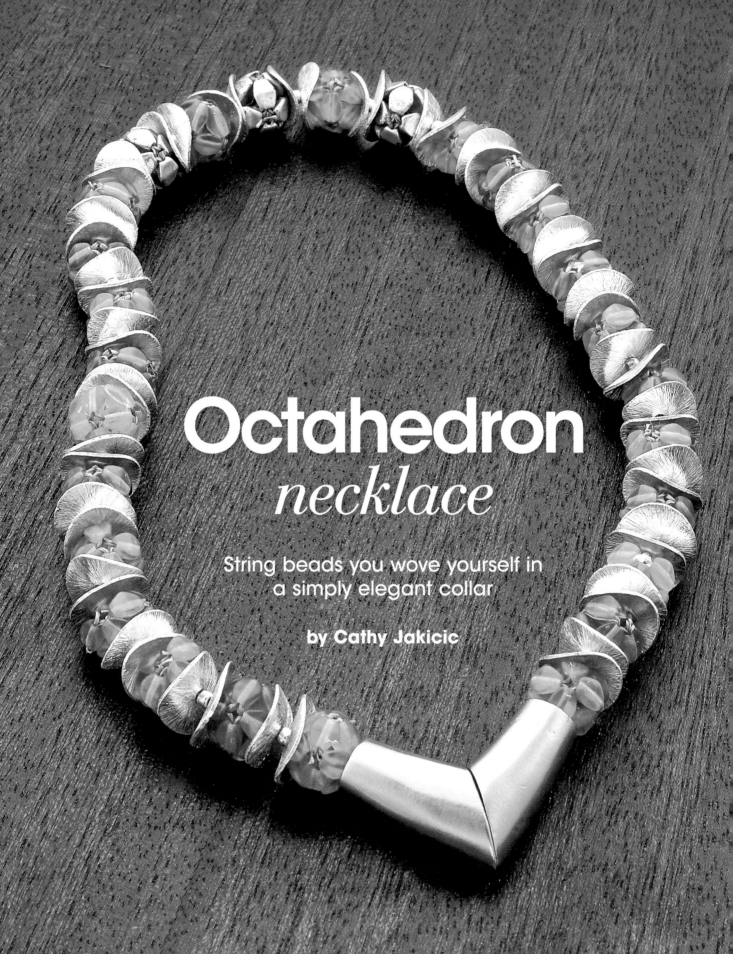

Octahedron
necklace

String beads you wove yourself in
a simply elegant collar

by Cathy Jakicic

Valerie Hector's Chinese bead-weaving class remains one of my favorites. I loved it! I thought I'd be a little overwhelmed, but I was energized by the class and couldn't wait to do more. The "starter" bead, the octahedron, is made from 12 beads woven into a sphere. I used 7 mm glass pinch beads to create my octahedrons, then strung them with silver spacers and a magnetic clasp in the front. If you're not up to the weaving, you can string any 10 mm round bead, but I urge you to try creating your own tiny sculptures. Your sense of accomplishment will match your sense of style.

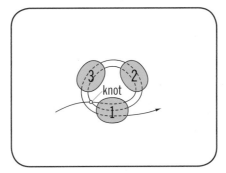

1 octahedron bead • Condition 24 in. (61 cm) of thread by pulling it through some beading wax. Thread a needle on one end. String three pinch beads and tie an overhand knot (Basics, p. 12), leaving a 2-in. (5 cm) tail. With the needle, go through beads 1, 2, 3, and 1. Pull the thread tight.

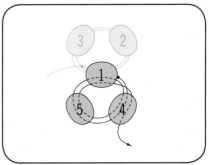

2 String beads 4 and 5. Go through beads 1, 4, 5, 1, and 4. Pull the thread tight.

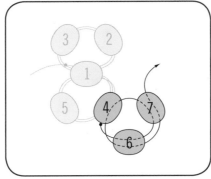

3 String beads 6 and 7. Go through beads 4, 6, and 7. Pull the thread tight.

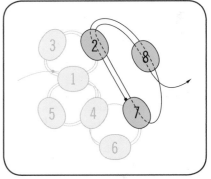

4 Go through bead 2. String bead 8 and go through beads 7, 2, and 8. Pull the thread tight.

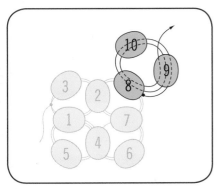

5 Turn the woven beads so the point formed by beads 1, 2, 7, and 4 faces down. String beads 9 and 10. Go through beads 8, 9, 10, 8, and 9. Pull the thread tight.

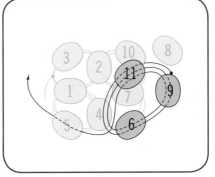

6 String bead 11. Go through beads 6, 9, 11, 6, 9, 11, and 5. Pull the thread tight.

Note: These octahedron instructions were adapted from Valerie's class instructions, which were based on Laura Shea's bead pattern.

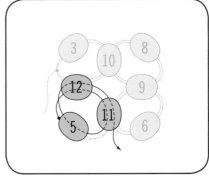

7 String bead 12 and go through bead 11. Pull the thread tight. Reinforce the octahedron by going through all of the beads until the structure is stiff. Follow the thread pattern through the beads. Do not go across the empty spaces between the beads. Trim the excess thread.

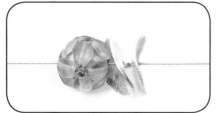

1 necklace • Cut a piece of beading wire (Basics). String an octahedron, a wavy spacer, a round spacer, and a wavy spacer. Repeat until the strand is within 1 in. (2.5 cm) of the finished length. End with an octahedron.

2 Check the fit, and add or remove beads if necessary. On one end, string a crimp bead and a 22-gauge jump ring. Go back through the beads just strung and tighten the wire. The jump ring is necessary so you can tighten the wire and still maintain a loop at the end of the strand. Crimp the crimp bead (Basics), trim the excess wire, and remove the jump ring. Repeat on the other end, making sure the beads are snug against each other.

3 Cut a 2-in. (5 cm) piece of 24-gauge wire. String the wire through one of the loops of beading wire and the two holes in half of the clasp. Pull the wire tight and twist the two ends together. Trim the excess wire. Repeat on the other end.

Supplies

one octahedron bead
- ◆ **12** 7 mm pinch beads
- ◆ One-G beading thread
- ◆ size 10 or 12 beading needle
- ◆ beading wax

necklace 14½ in. (36.8 cm)
- ◆ **27–30** 10 mm octahedron beads
- ◆ **52–58** 14 mm wavy spacers
- ◆ **26–29** 2 mm round spacers
- ◆ flexible beading wire, .014 or .015
- ◆ 4 in. (10 cm) 24-gauge half-hard wire
- ◆ 22-gauge jump ring
- ◆ **2** crimp beads
- ◆ magnetic V clasp
- ◆ chainnose or crimping pliers
- ◆ diagonal wire cutters

earrings
- ◆ **2** 10 mm octahedron beads
- ◆ **2** 14 mm wavy spacers
- ◆ **6** 2 mm round spacers
- ◆ **2** 2-in. (5 cm) head pins
- ◆ **2** 7 mm soldered jump rings
- ◆ pair of earring wires
- ◆ chainnose and roundnose pliers
- ◆ diagonal wire cutters

1 earrings • On a head pin, string a round spacer, a wavy spacer, an octahedron bead, and two round spacers. Make the first half of a wrapped loop (Basics).

2 Attach the bead unit to a jump ring and complete the wraps. Open the loop of an earring wire (Basics) and attach the dangle. Close the loop. Make a second earring.

Design alternative

Center a few octahedrons (made with glass bicone beads) on a chain to highlight your weaving prowess.

Tip

Practice making octahedrons by using 12 different colors of beads; bicones work well.

Two steps to style

Could-not-be-simpler earrings are gorgeous

by Irina Miech

I get so many compliments on these earrings, I don't have the heart to tell people how quick and simple they are. The only tricks are choosing beautiful materials and colors and fighting the temptation to make things fancy.

1 On a head pin, string a round crystal, a cone, and a bicone crystal. Make a wrapped loop (Basics, p. 12).

2 Open the loop of an earring wire (Basics). Attach the dangle and close the loop. Make a second earring.

Tip

The size of the opening (not the size of the cone itself) will determine how large a bead you'll need.

Design alternative

Try different cone and bead combinations for a virtually endless variety of looks.

Supplies

- **2** 20 mm cones
- **2** 8 mm round crystals
- **2** 3 mm bicone crystals
- **2** 2-in. (5 cm) head pins
- pair of earring wires
- chainnose and roundnose pliers
- diagonal wire cutters

Wire into perfect post

For no-fuss earrings, these spiral disks fit the bill

by Heather Boardman

With a few inches of wire and a pair of disk beads, you can whip up pretty post earrings in just a few minutes. In fact, these earrings are so easy to make, you may find yourself making a pair in every color.

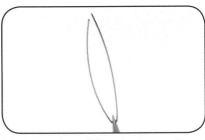

1 Cut a 4-in. (10 cm) piece of wire. Pull the ends of the wire together around the tip of your roundnose pliers to form an elongated U shape.

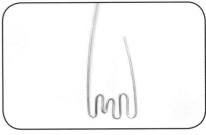

2 Bend the wire around your roundnose pliers to form three more U shapes.

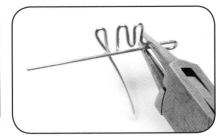

3 Pinch the base of each U together with the tip of your roundnose pliers. Pull each U around to form a clover shape.

"My favorite bead to make is the disk. So I'm always trying to come up with ways to showcase them." —HB

earrings

4 Bend each end to form a right angle. Hammer the clover on a bench block or anvil.

5 String a disk bead over both ends of the wire. With one end, make a coil around the other. Trim the excess wrapping wire.

6 Trim the remaining wire to ½ in. (1.3 cm) and file the end. Make a second earring.

Supplies

- **2** 15 mm disk beads
- 8 in. (20 cm) 20-gauge half-hard wire
- pair of metal ear nuts
- chainnose and roundnose pliers
- diagonal wire cutters
- bench block or anvil
- emery board or file
- hammer

Design alternative

For dangles, harness disk beads with a simple wire wrap. Use 24- or 26-gauge wire to make organic wraps with your fingers.

Tip

For more symmetrical wire shapes, form the wires for both earrings at the same time.

Ornamental

Follow a super-easy technique to make a custom wire bail

by Jessica Tiemens

This exotic lava bead was begging for something more than the usual wraps that accompany top-drilled beads. Add a few pearls and oval gemstones to keep the singularly bailed focal bead from being lonely.

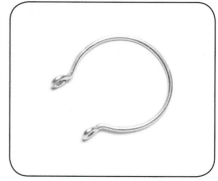

1 Cut a 2-in. (5 cm) piece of 24-gauge wire. Make a wrapped loop (Basics, p. 12) on one end. String a spacer, an oval bead, and a spacer and make a wrapped loop. Make three bead units.

2 Cut a 3-in. (7.6 cm) piece of 16-gauge wire. Wrap the wire around a cylindrical object. On each end, make a plain loop (Basics). Bend the loops.

3 Cut a 3½-in. (8.9 cm) piece of 24-gauge wire. String: pearl, loop of the 16-gauge wire, inverted teardrop bead, loop, pearl. Center the beads on the wire.

4 Wrap each end of the 24-gauge wire five times around the 16-gauge wire. Trim the excess.

bail

Supplies

necklace 19 in. (48 cm)

- ◆ 38 mm inverted teardrop bead
- ◆ **3** 8 mm oval beads
- ◆ **2** 6 mm rice pearls
- ◆ **6** 3 mm spacers
- ◆ 3 in. (7.6 cm) 16-gauge wire
- ◆ 9½ in. (24.1 cm) 24-gauge wire
- ◆ 28–32 in. (71–81 cm) chain, 3–4 mm links
- ◆ **4** 6 mm jump rings
- ◆ **2** 5 mm jump rings
- ◆ **2** 4 mm jump rings
- ◆ lobster claw clasp
- ◆ chainnose and roundnose pliers
- ◆ diagonal wire cutters
- ◆ ¾-in. (1.9 cm) diameter cylindrical object

5 Open two 4 mm jump rings (Basics) and attach each loop of a bead unit and the 16-gauge wire. Close the jump rings.

6 On each end of the bead unit, use a 6 mm jump ring to attach the 4 mm jump ring, 16-gauge wire, and another bead unit.

7 Cut two 14–16-in. (36–41 cm) pieces of chain. For each chain, open a link on one end and attach the other end. Close the link. On each end, use a 6 mm jump ring to attach the loop of a bead unit and a chain.

8 On one end, use a 5 mm jump ring to attach a lobster claw clasp. On the other end, attach a 5 mm jump ring.

Tips

- After attaching the first bead unit, you can gently curve the loops to help it hang more evenly from the 16-gauge wire.
- If you use soldered chain, you can use a jump ring to connect the ends in step 7 (instead of opening and closing links).

Cross ea

Flat beads make a flattering backdrop for your wirework ◆ by Ann Westby

I often see sterling silver or gold earrings with a swirl soldered onto the earring finding, and wanted to get that same look using a bead as a base. I figured out that I could attach the coil to a wire strung through the bead, placing the coil over the center of the bead, exactly where I wanted it. I bought my turquoise cross beads at a gem show, but any flat bead will work as a pretty showcase for the coil.

1 Cut a 5-in. (13 cm) piece of wire. On one end, use the tip of your roundnose pliers to make a tiny loop.

2 Grasp the loop with chainnose pliers and continue coiling the wire with your fingers. Make the coil about ⅜ in. (1 cm) in diameter. (Place it against a cross bead to determine the finished size.)

3 Make a right-angle bend centered above the coil. About ¼ in. (6 mm) from the bend, make a small wrapped loop (Basics, p. 12).

rrings

4 Grasp the wrapped loop with chainnose pliers and bend it at a right angle to the coil. Gently hammer both sides of the coil. If the coil loosens after hammering, adjust it with your fingers.

5 Cut a 2-in. (5 cm) piece of wire. Make a tiny loop on one end. String a cross bead and the coil. Make a wrapped loop.

6 Open the loop of an earring wire (Basics). Attach the dangle and close the loop. Make a second earring the mirror image of the first.

Design alternative

For bold earrings, I wrapped 20-gauge wire around the triangular end of a Fiskars Right Angle mandrel. I flattened the wraps slightly but didn't hammer them, and used a background of faceted amethysts.

Supplies

- **2** 20–25 mm cross or other flat beads
- 14 in. (36 cm) 20- or 22-gauge half-hard wire
- pair of earring wires
- chainnose and roundnose pliers
- diagonal wire cutters
- bench block or anvil
- hammer

Crystal & copper garden

Bead caps help
create a bouquet
of crystal buds.

Stamped and domed copper disks and colorful crystals represent Milwaukee's Domes

by Irina Miech

The Mitchell Park Horticultural Conservatory — "The Domes" — in Milwaukee is a plant lover's paradise, especially during a Wisconsin winter. This necklace, bracelet, and earrings use stamped copper domes, floral bead caps, and bold-colored bicones to express the juxtaposition of the geometric lines of The Domes and the organic nature of their exhibits.

The Domes are located at 524 S. Layton Blvd., Milwaukee, Wis.

1 necklace • Using a texture hammer, strike a copper disk to make stripes, turning the disk 45 degrees between each hit.

2 Holding the stamp at its base, use a hammer to make two or three floral impressions on the disk.

3 Center the disk face down in the appropriately sized indentation on a dapping block. Center the corresponding punch on the disk. Strike the punch with the hammer. Repeat as necessary.

4 Use hole-punch pliers to punch five holes along the edge of the domed disk: three at the bottom and two at the top.

5 On a head pin, string a 4–6 mm bicone crystal and make the first half of a wrapped loop (Basics, p. 12). Make 30 bicone units, adding bead caps to six to eight of the 6 mm units.

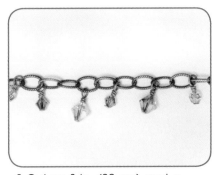

6 Cut an 8-in. (20 cm) and a 9¾-in. (24.8 cm) piece of chain. On each chain, open an end link and attach a top hole of the copper dome. Close the links. On each side of the dome, skip a link and attach a bicone unit. Attach bicone units to every other link, completing the wraps as you go. Attach six units to each side.

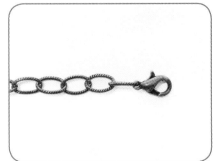

7 Cut two two-link pieces of chain and one four-link piece of chain. Attach three bicone units to each of the shorter chains and nine bicone units to the longer chain.

8 Open an end link on each of the chains and attach a hole at the bottom of the pendant. Close the links.

9 On the end of the 8-in. (20 cm) chain, open the link and attach a lobster claw clasp. Close the link. On the end of the 9¾-in. (24.8 cm) chain, attach a 4 mm bicone unit and complete the wraps.

1 bracelet • Following necklace step 5, make 36 bicone units, half with bead caps. Complete the wraps on each unit. Open a jump ring (Basics) and attach six bicone units. Close the jump ring. Make six clusters.

2 Following necklace steps 1, 2, and 3, make five copper domes. On each dome, use hole-punch pliers to punch two holes opposite each other. Using jump rings, link the domes and clusters.

3 On each end, use a jump ring to attach half of a toggle clasp.

Adding a patina

I gave the detailing on the copper domes some extra dimension by using liver of sulfur to create a patina and then polishing the color off the surface, leaving only the indentations darkened. For a demonstration of the patination process, watch *Art Jewelry* Associate Editor Jill Erickson's video on ArtJewelryMag.com or YouTube.com. Search for "liver of sulfur patina."

Supplies

all projects
- chainnose and roundnose pliers
- diagonal wire cutters
- ball-peen hammer or mallet
- bench block or anvil
- dapping kit
- **1** or **2** floral-themed stamps
- metal hole-punch pliers
- stripe texture hammer
- liver of sulfur and polishing cloth or brush (optional)

necklace 17 in. (43 cm)
- 26 mm round copper disk
- **30** 4–6 mm bicone crystals in various colors
- **6–8** 6 mm floral bead caps
- 20 in. (51 cm) cable chain, 8 mm links
- **30** 1½-in. (3.8 cm) head pins
- lobster claw clasp

bracelet
- **5** 26 mm round copper disks
- **36** 4–6 mm bicone crystals in various colors
- **18** 6 mm floral bead caps
- **18** 7 mm jump rings
- **36** 1½-in. (3.8 cm) head pins
- toggle clasp

earrings
- **2** 26 mm round copper disks
- **2** 6 mm bicone crystals
- **2** 6 mm floral bead caps
- **2** links cable chain, 8 mm links
- **2** 1½-in. (3.8 cm) head pins
- **2** 7 mm jump rings
- pair of earring wires

1 earrings • Following necklace steps 1, 2, and 3, make two copper domes. On each dome, use hole-punch pliers to punch two holes opposite each other. Following necklace step 5, make two bicone units with a bead cap. Attach a bicone unit to a chain link and complete the wraps. Open a jump ring (Basics) and attach the dangle to a dome. Close the jump ring.

2 Open the loop of an earring wire (Basics) and attach the dangle. Close the loop. Make a second earring.

Tips

- If you don't want to purchase an entire dapping kit, a dapping block (and punch) with a 28 mm depression will work.
- If you don't use chain with open links, you'll need three 7 mm jump rings to attach the necklace's clasp and dome pendant.
- To lengthen the bracelet, attach extra jump rings on each end.

"The colors in the crystals and the floral bead caps represent bright blooms." —IM

Glass, cera

mic, & pearls

Beads capture Italian flavor

The sun-drenched colors of this bracelet and earrings bring back warm memories

by Cathy Jakicic

Italy is an emotional rather than a geographical home for me. My mother's family is Italian, and I've enjoyed two glorious visits so far. The colors of this bracelet-and-earrings set recall the warmth of the people and the majesty of the art. The Venetian beads are a reminder of my favorite city, and the clasp also reminds me of Venice. When I fed the pigeons in Piazza San Marco, a half-dozen perched on my arms and shoulders waiting for the next morsel. Even the birds made me feel at home!

1 bracelet • Cut a piece of beading wire (Basics, p. 12). On the wire, center: bicone crystal, bead cap, 36 mm Venetian bead, bead cap, bicone.

2 On each end, string: 10 mm bead, bicone, 15 mm Venetian bead, bicone, 10 mm. String the pattern from step 1.

3 On each end, string a crimp bead, a bicone, and half of a clasp. Check the fit, and add or remove beads if necessary. Go back through the beads just strung and tighten the wire. Crimp the crimp bead (Basics) and trim the excess wire.

❝For me, the work of Venetian bead artisans is incomparable.❞ —CJ

Color notes

The Venetian beads are rubino. The bicone crystals are light amethyst dorado.

To make "drip" beads, bead makers use exposed gold and colored translucent glass to create a textured pattern that resembles dripping glass.

Supplies

bracelet
- ◆ **2–3** 36 mm oval Venetian beads
- ◆ **2–5** 15 mm Venetian lentil beads
- ◆ **4** 10 mm metal accent beads
- ◆ **6** 8 mm bead caps
- ◆ **12** 4 mm bicone crystals
- ◆ flexible beading wire, .014 or .015
- ◆ **2** crimp beads
- ◆ toggle clasp
- ◆ chainnose or crimping pliers
- ◆ diagonal wire cutters

earrings
- ◆ **2** 15 mm Venetian lentil beads
- ◆ **2** 4 mm bicone crystals
- ◆ **2** 13 mm hammered rings
- ◆ **2** 1½-in. (3.8 cm) eye pins
- ◆ **2** 5 mm jump rings
- ◆ pair of earring wires
- ◆ chainnose and roundnose pliers
- ◆ diagonal wire cutters

1 earrings • On an eye pin, string a 15 mm Venetian bead and a bicone crystal. Make a wrapped loop (Basics).

2 Open a jump ring (Basics) and attach a 13 mm hammered ring and the Venetian-bead unit. Close the jump ring.

3 Open the loop of an earring wire (Basics). Attach the dangle and close the loop. Make a second earring.

Tips

• For a shorter bracelet, string just two oval beads and five lentil beads.
• Varying the warm metal tones gives the bracelet and earrings extra depth. Try mixing different shades of copper, gold, antique gold, rose gold, or brass.

Trade bead treasures

Understanding the origins of African beads allows you to appreciate this jewelry even more

by Jane Konkel

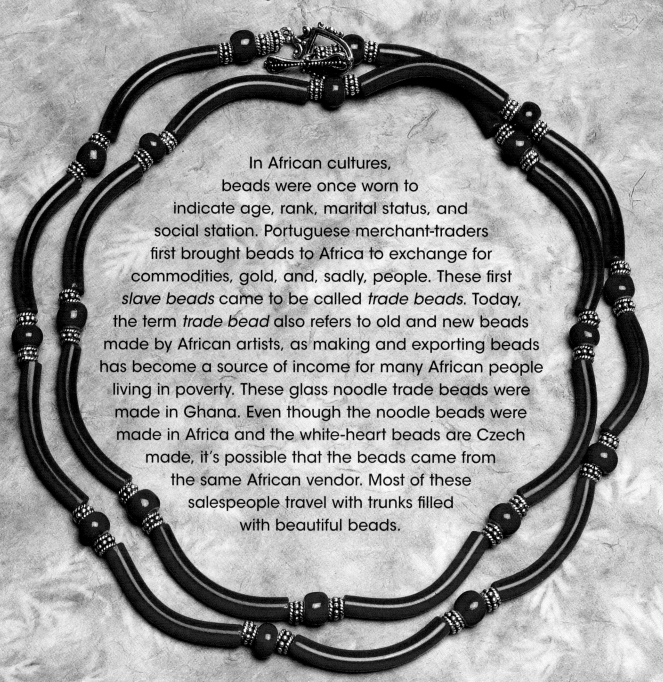

In African cultures, beads were once worn to indicate age, rank, marital status, and social station. Portuguese merchant-traders first brought beads to Africa to exchange for commodities, gold, and, sadly, people. These first *slave beads* came to be called *trade beads*. Today, the term *trade bead* also refers to old and new beads made by African artists, as making and exporting beads has become a source of income for many African people living in poverty. These glass noodle trade beads were made in Ghana. Even though the noodle beads were made in Africa and the white-heart beads are Czech made, it's possible that the beads came from the same African vendor. Most of these salespeople travel with trunks filled with beautiful beads.

Supplies

necklace 32 in. (81 cm)

- 24-in. (61 cm) strand 35 mm glass noodle beads
- **27–47** 7 mm white-heart beads
- **18–28** 5 mm spacers
- flexible beading wire, .014 or .015
- **2** crimp beads
- toggle clasp
- chainnose or crimping pliers
- diagonal wire cutters

three bracelets

- 24-in. (61 cm) strand 23 mm glass noodle beads
- **17–19** 7 mm white-heart beads
- **34–42** 5 mm spacers
- flexible beading wire, .014 or .015
- ribbon elastic
- diagonal wire cutters
- G-S Hypo Cement
- scissors

A bead's color, condition, and stringing material offer clues to its origin. These smooth, clean, red beads, originally strung on raffia, are most likely new.

1 necklace • Cut a piece of beading wire (Basics, p. 12). String: spacer, 7 mm bead, spacer, noodle bead. Repeat until the strand is within 1 in. (2.5 cm) of the finished length.

2 On each end, attach half of a toggle clasp (Basics).

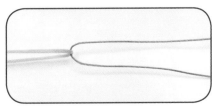

1 three bracelets • For each bracelet, cut a 24–28-in. (61–71 cm) piece of ribbon elastic. Cut a 3-in. (7.6 cm) piece of beading wire and fold it in half, centering the elastic around the fold to create a needle.

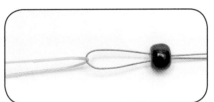

2 String beads and spacers as desired until the strand is the finished length.

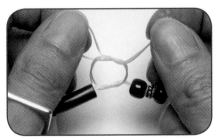

3 Tie a surgeon's knot (Basics). Apply glue to the knot and trim the excess elastic.

Tip

After you tie and glue the knots for each bracelet, gently pull the elastic to hide each knot inside a noodle bead.

Dripping
with style

Matte silver contrasts beautifully with shimmering glass.

Droplets of glass add color to a fluid bracelet and earrings

by Laurie-Anne Clinton

This simple bracelet requires nothing more opening and closing jump rings and an eye for color. Oval jump rings lend the beads a bit of wiggle room that gives the bracelet that extra swing.

1 bracelet • Cut a 7–8-in. (18–20 cm) piece of chain. Open a jump ring (Basics, p. 12). Attach a teardrop bead to the fourth link of the chain. Close the jump ring. Use a jump ring to attach another teardrop to the same link.

2 Attach two teardrops to every other link, leaving a few links open at the end. Use a jump ring to attach a pendant to the next open link.

3 On one end, use a jump ring to attach a lobster claw clasp and the chain. On the other end, attach a jump ring.

1 earrings • Open a 7 mm jump ring (Basics). Attach a teardrop bead to a circle pendant. Close the jump ring. Attach a total of six teardrops.

2 Use a 6 mm jump ring to attach the dangle and the loop of an earring post. Make a second earring.

Supplies

bracelet
- 22 x 27 mm poppy pendant
- **30–34** 10 mm glass teardrop beads
- 7–8 in. (18–20 cm) rolo chain, 8 mm links
- **30–34** 9 mm oval jump rings
- lobster claw clasp
- chainnose and roundnose pliers, or **2** pairs of chainnose pliers
- diagonal wire cutters

earrings
- **2** 29 mm circle pendants
- **12** 10 mm glass teardrop beads
- **12** 7 mm jump rings
- **2** 6 mm jump rings
- pair of hammered earring posts with loop, plus ear nuts
- chainnose and roundnose pliers, or **2** pairs of chainnose pliers

Tip

Make sure you use a large enough lobster claw clasp for the scale and weight of the bracelet. I used a 14 mm clasp.

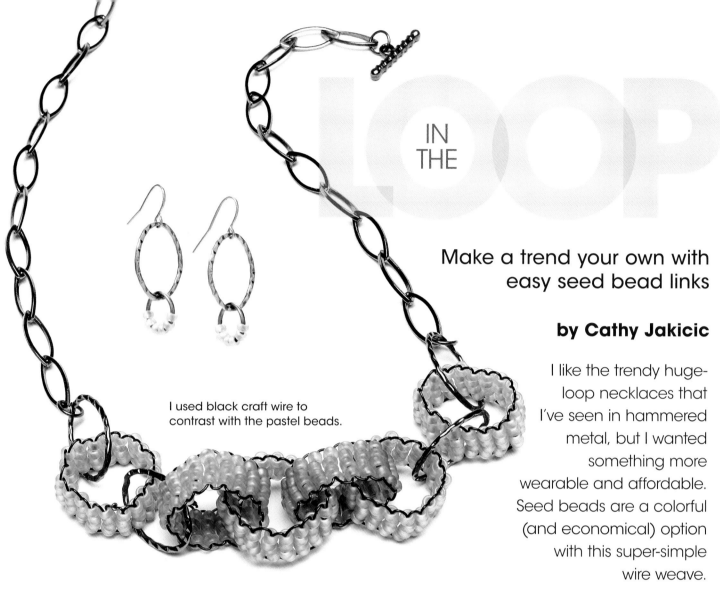

Make a trend your own with easy seed bead links

by Cathy Jakicic

I like the trendy huge-loop necklaces that I've seen in hammered metal, but I wanted something more wearable and affordable. Seed beads are a colorful (and economical) option with this super-simple wire weave.

I used black craft wire to contrast with the pastel beads.

1 necklace • Cut an 18-in. (46 cm) piece of wire. Center four seed beads.

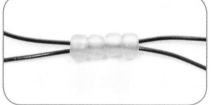

2 On one end, string four seed beads. Bring the other end of the wire through the four new seed beads from the opposite direction.

3 a Pull both ends of the wire until the rows are next to each other.
b Repeat steps 2 to 3a for a total of 19 rows.

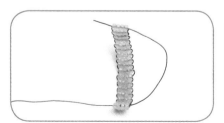

4 Bring one wire end through the first row of beads.

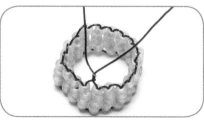

5 Tighten the wire so the first and last rows are next to each other. Twist the wire tails together twice. Trim the wire and fold it to the inside of the loop.

6 Follow steps 1 to 3a to start another loop. Connect the first loop, then follow steps 4 and 5.

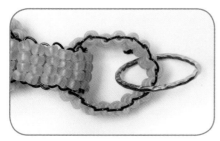

7 On each end, weave another loop and connect it to an oval link.

8 On each end, weave another loop to connect another oval link.

9 Cut two 6–7-in. (15–18 cm) pieces of chain. On each end of the bead-and-link segment, open a jump ring (Basics, p. 12) and attach the oval link and a piece of chain. Close the jump ring.

10 On each end, use a jump ring to attach half of a toggle clasp.

1 earrings • Open a jump ring (Basics). String six seed beads. Attach the jump ring to an oval link. Close the jump ring.

2 Open the loop of an earring wire (Basics). Attach the dangle and close the loop. Make a second earring.

Supplies

necklace 18 in. (46 cm)
- 14 g 8º seed beads
- **4** 20 mm oval links
- 3 yd. (2.8 m) 24-gauge craft wire
- 12–14 in. (30–36 cm) marquise-shape chain, 14 mm links
- **4** 7 mm jump rings
- toggle clasp
- chainnose and roundnose pliers, or **2** pairs of chainnose pliers
- diagonal wire cutters

earrings
- **12** 8º seed beads
- **2** 20 mm oval links
- **2** 10 mm jump rings
- pair of earring wires
- chainnose and roundnose pliers, or **2** pairs of chainnose pliers

Tip

If you'd rather use beading thread to weave the seed beads, cut the thread three times longer than the wire. Then, weave the excess in and out of the rows so the loop holds its shape.

Design alternative

Skip the chain and go with an all-beaded design. One tube of 8º seed beads makes about six loops, so you'll need two tubes for a bracelet.

Crocheted
necklace

Seashells are tied to beach memories

by Kim St. Jean

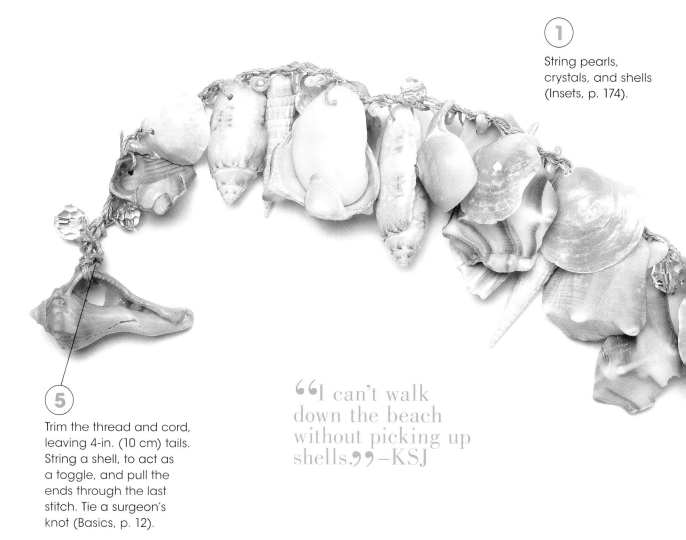

1

String pearls, crystals, and shells (Insets, p. 174).

5

Trim the thread and cord, leaving 4-in. (10 cm) tails. String a shell, to act as a toggle, and pull the ends through the last stitch. Tie a surgeon's knot (Basics, p. 12).

66I can't walk down the beach without picking up shells.99—KSJ

Nothing says Myrtle Beach, S.C., like seashells, and nothing says Kim St. Jean like tools. If I'm not hammering or sawing in my workshop, I'm on vacation, searching the beach for something to take back home to drill. My son and I collected these shells at a campground. After drilling them, I used bead crochet to display my handiwork.

2 Chain stitch one end of the thread and cord (Insets).

6 Make the loop half of the finishing (Insets).

3 Continue to chain stitch, sliding down pearls and crystals every other stitch, to cover about 2 in. (5 cm).

4 Continue to chain stitch, sliding down shells, pearls, and crystals every other stitch until the beaded segment is about 15 in. (38 cm) long.

See Techniques and Insets to learn how to make Kim's necklace.

Tips for drilling shells

• Use a drill that will turn in slow revolutions. I use my drill press set at 1100 rpms. In most cases, a Dremel-style tool will go too fast even on the lowest speed.
• Use a titanium nitride coated drill bit from the hardware store. The ones I use cost about $2 for 10 bits.
• Drill shells underwater. Submerge the item to be drilled on a small piece of wood and lower the drill bit to the spot you wish to drill.
• Start the drill moving very slowly and apply light pressure. Let the drill bit do the work.

Techniques

 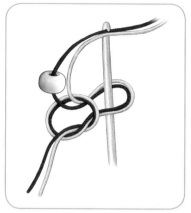

chain stitch • Make a loop in the cords, crossing the ends over the tails. Insert a crochet hook in the loop. Bring the cords over the hook, and pull them through the loop. Repeat for the desired number of stitches.

bead chain stitch • Slide the first bead to the crochet hook and chain stitch into the next stitch. Make sure the bead hangs freely. Repeat for the desired number of stitches.

Insets

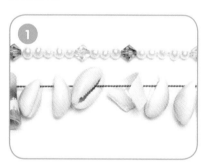

1

String 8 in. (20 cm) of pearls and crystals on silk knotting thread. String 8 in. (20 cm) of shells on C-Lon knotting cord. You can string more as you go.

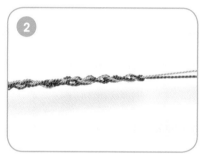

2

Leave a 4-in. (10 cm) tail. Chain enough stitches (Techniques) to cover about 2 in. (5 cm) of thread and cord.

6

Use roundnose pliers or a crochet hook to pull the ends through the stitch adjacent to the first bead to form a loop. Tie a surgeon's knot (Basics).

Supplies

necklace 18 in. (46 cm)
- **28–34** seashells, top drilled
- **8–10** 6–8 mm crystals
- **36–46** 4–6 mm pearls, top drilled

- C-Lon knotting cord
- silk knotting thread
- diagonal wire cutters
- crochet hook (Boye size E/4-3.50MM)

Roman glass is shards from jars, goblets, and other vessels.

Roman GLASS

Ancient glass makes beautiful contemporary jewelry

by Jane Konkel

In 2006, this Roman glass, which is estimated to be between 900 to 1200 years old, was excavated from the Nimroz province of Afghanistan. Similar ancient glass has been found in northern Africa. The typical shades of blue and green come from different mineral impurities in the sand during the time the glass was made, and the surface iridescence resulted from oxidation over time. I like the simplicity of the disks, so I added old glass cylinder beads and knotted them on thread in two colors.

1 necklace • Cut a 36-in. (.9 m) piece of braiding string. Cut another piece in a second color. Over both pieces, center a pendant and tie an overhand knot (Basics, p. 12).

2 Over all four ends, string a 3 mm bead and tie an overhand knot. On each side, pair a string of each color.

3 On each side, string each end in opposite directions through a disk. Bring the strings around the top of the bead. Tie an overhand knot with each pair.

4 a String a 3 mm and tie a knot.
b Repeat steps 3 and 4a until the beaded section is within 10 in. (25 cm) of the finished length.

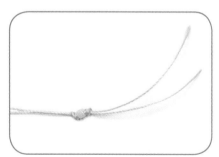

5 On each side, tie a knot about 2 in. (5 cm) from each end. String a 3 mm and tie a knot. Trim the excess string. Tie a bow to wear.

"I loved the way these beads came strung on simple thread. I wanted to add a little color and some knots for an unaffected look."
—JK

Supplies

necklace 34 in. (86 cm)
- 25–35 mm Roman glass pendant
- **6–10** 15–20 mm Roman glass disk beads
- **8–12** 3 mm glass cylinder beads
- 36 in. (.9 m) braiding string in **2 colors**
- scissors

earrings
- **2** 15–20 mm Roman glass disk beads
- **2** 3 mm glass cylinder beads
- **2** 7 mm bead caps
- **2** 2½-in. (6.4 cm) decorative head pins
- **2** 5 mm jump rings
- pair of twisted-wire earring wires (Turtle Island Beads, turtleisland-beads.com)
- chainnose and roundnose pliers
- diagonal wire cutters
- bench block or anvil
- hammer

Tips

- Braiding string is also called braiding thread.
- The original beads are strung on cotton cord with beads or knots between them. The beads range in size and thickness, with 20–25 beads and one pendant per strand.

1 earrings • On a decorative head pin, string a 3 mm bead, a bead cap, and a disk. Bend the wire up at a right angle to the disk.

2 Hammer both sides of the head pin and both sides of a jump ring.

Design alternative

Arrange disks in a blossoming ring to use up leftover or mismatched beads.

3 Position your roundnose pliers 1 in. (2.5 cm) from the end of the head pin and pull the wire over the pliers. Wrap the end around the stem between the bead cap and disk.

4 Open the jump ring (Basics) and attach the dangle and the loop of an earring wire. Close the jump ring. Make a second earring.

"I love how the ceramic and metal textures play off of each other." —IM

Bee stylish

Ceramic and brass components create a fashion buzz

by Irina Miech

When I saw that Clay River Designs and Vintaj Natural Brass Co. both created bee-themed components, I knew I had to put them together. The honey-toned colors and design are subtle so it doesn't feel like I'm going overboard with a too-cute theme.

1 bracelet • On an eye pin, string a 6 mm rondelle and make a plain loop (Basics, p. 12). Make eight bead units.

2 Open one loop of a bead unit (Basics) and attach it to a loop of a bee connector. Close the loop. Repeat for each loop of the connector.

Cut two five-link chains and attach each chain to a loop of a rondelle unit as shown. Use a rondelle unit to attach both chain ends. Make a second bee unit.

3 On each end of the bracelet blank, open a jump ring (Basics) and connect the blank and a bee unit. Close the jump ring.

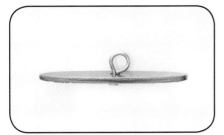

4 On a head pin, string a toggle bar and make a plain loop.

5 Cut a three- to five-link piece of chain. On one end of the chain, attach the toggle bar's loop. On the other end of the chain, attach a rondelle unit. Attach the hammered ring to the other rondelle unit.

1 earrings • On a head pin, string a rondelle and make a plain loop (Basics). Open the loop and attach the bead unit to a bee connector's bottom loop.

2 Cut a 1½-in. (3.8 cm) piece of chain. Attach a split ring to each end.

3 Attach each split ring to an outer loop of the bee.

4 Open a jump ring (Basics) and attach the middle link of chain and the loop of an earring post. Close the jump ring. Make a second earring.

Supplies

bracelet
- 1¾-in. (4.4 cm) ceramic bracelet blank
- **2** 18 x 20 mm bee connectors
- **8** 6 mm rondelles
- 3 in. (7.6 cm) cable chain, 4 mm links
- 1½-in. (3.8 cm) head pin
- **8** 1½-in. (3.8 cm) eye pins
- **2** 9.5 mm etched jump rings
- 30 mm engraved toggle bar
- 22 mm hammered ring
- chainnose and roundnose pliers
- diagonal wire cutters

earrings
- **2** 18 x 20 mm bee connectors
- **2** 6 mm rondelles
- 3¼ in. (8.3 cm) cable chain, 4 mm links
- **2** 1½-in. (3.8 cm) head pins
- **4** 6 mm split rings
- **2** 4 mm jump rings
- pair of earring posts with loop, plus ear nuts
- chainnose and roundnose pliers
- diagonal wire cutters
- split-ring pliers (optional)

Design alternative

Allergic to bees? Bend a filigree component into a curved bracelet blank.

Disk-and-coil EARRINGS

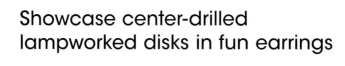

Showcase center-drilled lampworked disks in fun earrings

by Heather Boardman

Have fun making organic-looking wraps — no need for the coils to be the same size or perfectly parallel. For the widest part of the coils, I wrapped wire around a standard Bic pen. For smaller coils, try a knitting needle.

1 blue-and-purple earrings • Cut a 7-in. (18 cm) piece of wire. String a disk. About 1¼ in. (3.2 cm) from one end, bend the wire around the disk. Wrap the short wire around the longer wire and trim the excess.

2 Wrap the wire around a pen barrel or knitting needle three to five times. Use your fingers to adjust the coils.

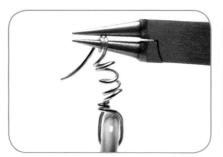

3 Wrap the wire around the jaw of your roundnose pliers twice, making two loops parallel to the disk. Trim the excess wire.

4 Open the loop of an earring wire (Basics, p. 12). Attach the dangle and close the loop. Make a second earring.

1 green earrings • Cut a 9-in. (23 cm) piece of wire. Follow steps 1 and 2 of the blue-and-purple earrings. Bend the wire upward at a right angle, centering it above the coils. Wrap the wire around a mandrel or other cylindrical object to make an earring wire. Trim the excess wire.

2 About ⅛ in. (3 mm) from the end, bend the wire upward with chainnose pliers. File the end. Make a second earring.

Tip

Create a pendant by making the top loops perpendicular (instead of parallel) to the disk bead. Separate the loops to make a bail.

Supplies

blue-and-purple earrings

- **2** 15–20 mm disk beads, center drilled
- 14 in. (36 cm) 20-gauge half-hard wire
- pair of earring wires
- chainnose and roundnose pliers
- diagonal wire cutters
- round-barreled pen, knitting needle, or other cylindrical object

green earrings

- **2** 15–20 mm disk beads, center drilled
- 18 in. (46 cm) 20-gauge half-hard wire
- chainnose and roundnose pliers
- diagonal wire cutters
- metal file or emery board
- round-barreled pen, knitting needle, or other cylindrical object
- Fiskars Right Angle mandrel (optional)

Try crystals in colors to match the icing on the doughnuts and cupcakes.

Bakery bracelet

Try this sweet jewelry treat ◆ by Toni Plastino

If you resolved to ban sweets from your diet, here's a delicious loophole. A colorful pastry bracelet is as simple to make as it is tempting to look at. Glue doughnuts to the disks on a bracelet form and dangle crystals and cupcakes from the loops. No calories or crumbs make this bijou bakery a guilt-free pleasure. So go ahead — indulge.

1 bracelet • On a head pin, string a spacer and a cupcake bead. Make a wrapped loop (Basics, p. 12). On a head pin, string a crystal. Make a wrapped loop. Make one of each unit for each loop of the bracelet form.

2 Open a jump ring (Basics) and attach a cupcake unit to a chain link. Close the jump ring. Use jump rings to attach alternating crystal units and cupcake units.

3 Dot a disk with glue and apply a doughnut bead. Repeat with the remaining disks.

❝When inspiration hits, sketch it out before you lose it.❞ TP

1 earrings • On a head pin, string a spacer and a cupcake bead. Make the first half of a wrapped loop (Basics).

2 Trim the head from a head pin and make a plain loop on one end (Basics). String a crystal and make a plain loop. Repeat with a doughnut bead, making the second loop perpendicular to the first.

Supplies

bracelet
- ◆ **6–11** 10 mm cupcake beads
- ◆ **7–11** 10 mm doughnut beads
- ◆ **7–11** 6 mm crystals
- ◆ **7–11** 3 mm round spacers
- ◆ disk-and-loop bracelet form
- ◆ **14–22** 1½-in. (3.8 cm) head pins
- ◆ **14–22** 5 mm jump rings
- ◆ chainnose and roundnose pliers
- ◆ diagonal wire cutters
- ◆ Super New Glue or Dazzle Tac adhesive

earrings
- ◆ **2** 10 mm cupcake beads
- ◆ **2** 10 mm doughnut beads
- ◆ **2** 6 mm crystals
- ◆ **2** 3 mm flat spacers
- ◆ **6** 1½-in. (3.8 cm) head pins
- ◆ pair of decorative earring wires
- ◆ chainnose and roundnose pliers
- ◆ diagonal wire cutters

Cupcake and doughnut beads from Rings & Things (rings-things. com)

3 Attach the loop of the cupcake unit to a loop of the doughnut unit. Complete the wraps. Open the loop of the crystal unit (Basics) and attach the doughnut unit's remaining loop. Close the loop.

4 Open the loop of an earring wire and attach the dangle. Close the loop. Make a second earring.

Supply notes

• The disk-and-loop bracelet forms are available in several lengths. When ordering, check the number of disks and loops, then order the appropriate number of cupcake and doughnut beads.
• The crystal color used in the gunmetal bracelet is Indian pink. In the silver bracelet, I used topaz and tanzanite.

Design alternative

Really sweet on doughnuts? Use larger 22 mm doughnuts in your bracelet.

METALLIC
multistrand

I used seven kinds of seed beads in this six-strander. Because the drop beads have a strong impact on the overall look of the necklace (and are available in fewer colors), choose those first. Then, after you've gathered a collection of colors, string one-inch sections, changing the order of the sections from strand to strand. To wear, let the necklace fall naturally or twist the strands for a ropelike effect.

①

necklace • Cut six pieces of beading wire (Basics, p. 12). On each wire, string 1 in. (2.5 cm) of seed beads or drop beads, then a spacer. Repeat, varying the order of the sections, until each strand is within 2 in. (5 cm) of the finished length. Make sure to begin and end with smaller seed beads (they'll fit inside the cones more easily).

Stagger segments of seed beads in a dimensional necklace

by Irina Miech

"I wanted to create a set that goes with anything, no matter what your metal preference."
–IM

Finish the ends with cones and a hook-and-eye clasp (Technique, p. 186).

For visual interest, string spacers in one metal and the clasp and cones in another.

Supplies

necklace 18½–19 in. (47–48 cm)
- seed beads
  - tube 3.4 mm drop beads
  - **2** tubes 8º s, in two colors
  - tube 10º triangle beads
  - hank 11º Charlottes, metallic
  - hank 13º Charlottes, purple or bronze
  - hank 13º Charlottes, mixed silver and gold
- **90–110** 4 mm flat spacers
- flexible beading wire, .014 or .015
- 8 in. (20 cm) 22-gauge half-hard wire
- **2** cones
- **6** crimp beads
- hook-and-eye clasp
- chainnose and roundnose pliers
- diagonal wire cutters
- crimping pliers (optional)

earrings
- seed beads
  - **6** 3.4 mm drop beads
  - **4** 10º triangle beads
- **2** 12 mm oval links
- **2** 2-in. (5 cm) decorative head pins
- pair of earring wires
- chainnose and roundnose pliers
- diagonal wire cutters

earrings • For
each earring:
On a decorative
head pin, string
seed beads. Make
the first half of
a wrapped loop
(Basics). Attach a
link, complete the
wraps, and attach
an earring wire.

Design alternative

Make a monochromatic bracelet with leftover
Charlottes. String 11°s and add large-hole spacers
that slide over the seed beads.

Technique: Finishing with cones

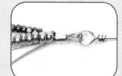

1. Cut a 4-in.
(10 cm) piece of
22-gauge wire.
Make a wrapped
loop on one end
(Basics).

2. Over a pair of
wires, string a
crimp bead and
the wrapped loop.
Go back through
the crimp bead
and tighten the
wires. Repeat with
the remaining
pairs of wires.

3. Repeat steps
1 and 2 on the
other ends of the
wires. Check the
fit, and add or
remove beads if
necessary. Crimp
the crimp beads
(Basics) and trim
the excess wire.

4. On each end,
string a cone and
a 10°. Make the
first half of a
wrapped loop.

5. On each end,
attach half of a
clasp. Complete
the wraps.

Tips

• For quicker stringing,
transfer seed beads directly
from the strand onto your
beading wire.
• Try base metal spacers as
an economical alternative
to vermeil or gold-filled.

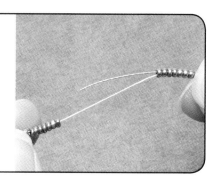

String a summer
necklace and earrings
in natural tones

by Tammy Powley

Memories
of the
beach

Supplies

necklace 21½ in. (54.6 cm)
- 20 mm crystal starfish pendant
- **12–15** 15–20 mm stick pearls, center drilled
- 16-in. (41 cm) 8 mm faceted round mother-of-pearl beads
- **12–14** 6 mm bicone crystals
- **9–12** 4 mm round crystals
- **24–28** 6 mm flat spacers
- 14 mm textured ring
- flexible beading wire, .014 or .015
- 6–7 mm jump ring
- **4** crimp beads
- **4** crimp covers
- spring-ring or lobster claw clasp, plus soldered jump ring or figure-8 connector
- chainnose and roundnose pliers, or **2** pairs of chainnose pliers
- crimping pliers
- diagonal wire cutters

earrings
- **2** 15–20 mm stick pearls, center drilled
- **2** 8 mm faceted round mother-of-pearl beads, left over from necklace
- **4** 6 mm bicone crystals
- **4** 4 mm round crystals
- **2** 6 mm flat spacers
- 6 in. (15 cm) 24-gauge half-hard wire
- **6** 1½-in. (3.8 cm) head pins
- pair of earring wires
- chainnose and roundnose pliers
- diagonal wire cutters

Living in south Florida, I see an abundance of color all around me. But I also find inspiration in the soothing palette offered by local beaches. To represent the elements of sand and sea, I opted for mother-of-pearl, white biwa (stick) pearls, and aquamarine crystals.

1 necklace • Open a jump ring (Basics, p. 12). Attach a starfish pendant and a textured ring and close the jump ring.

2 Cut two 14–16-in. (36–41 cm) pieces of beading wire. On one wire, string a crimp bead and the ring. Go back through the crimp bead and tighten the wire. Make a folded crimp (Basics).

3 String: spacer, bicone crystal, spacer, five stick pearls alternated with four round crystals, spacer, bicone, spacer, four 8 mm faceted beads. Repeat until the strand is within 1 in. (2.5 cm) of half the finished length.

4 Attach the second wire to the ring as in step 2. String a spacer, a bicone, a spacer, and five 8 mms. String: spacer, bicone, spacer, three 8 mms, repeating until the strand is within 1 in. (2.5 cm) of half the finished length.

5 On one end, attach half of a clasp (Basics). Repeat on the other end, substituting a soldered jump ring or figure-8 connector for the clasp.

6 Close a crimp cover over each crimp.

1 earrings • On a head pin, string an 8 mm faceted bead and a spacer. Make a wrapped loop (Basics). On a head pin, string a bicone crystal. Make a plain loop (Basics). Make a second bicone unit.

2 Cut a 3-in. (7.6 cm) piece of wire. Make the first half of a wrapped loop. String a round crystal, a stick pearl, and a round crystal. Make the first half of a wrapped loop.

3 On one loop of the pearl unit, attach a bicone unit, the 8 mm bead unit, and a bicone unit. Complete the wraps.

4 Attach the dangle and the loop of an earring wire. Complete the wraps. Make a second earring.

One superlong necklace
offers multiple looks

by Naomi Fujimoto

For balanced style,
wear both short
and long strands.

Pearls extend your
style options

By stringing crystals with four or five strands of pearls, you can make a necklace more than six feet long. And you won't need a clasp — simply wrap the pearls however the mood strikes you.

Supplies

necklace 75 in. (1.9 m)
- **4–5** 16-in. (41 cm) strands 9–12 mm pearls
- **140–160** 3 mm crystals
- 3 mm spacer
- flexible beading wire, .014 or .015
- **2** crimp beads
- chainnose or crimping pliers
- diagonal wire cutters

earrings
- **2** 9–12 mm pearls
- **2** 3 mm crystals
- **2** 1½-in. (3.8 cm) head pins
- pair of earring wires
- chainnose and roundnose pliers
- diagonal wire cutters

1 necklace • Cut a piece of beading wire (Basics, p. 12). String a pearl and a crystal, repeating until the necklace is the finished length.

2 On each end, string a crystal and a crimp bead. String each end through a spacer in opposite directions. Go through the beads just strung. Tighten the wire and crimp the crimp bead (Basics). Trim the excess wire.

1 earrings • On a head pin, string a pearl and a crystal. Make a plain loop (Basics).

2 Open the loop of an earring wire (Basics) and attach the dangle. Close the loop. Make a second earring.

Tip

To lower your project costs, substitute 8º or 11º seed beads for the crystals.

Design alternative

I used a strand of mixed quartz and chalcedony for a fun alternative to the sophisticated pearls. Make sure the stones aren't too big — six feet of beads can really weigh a girl down.

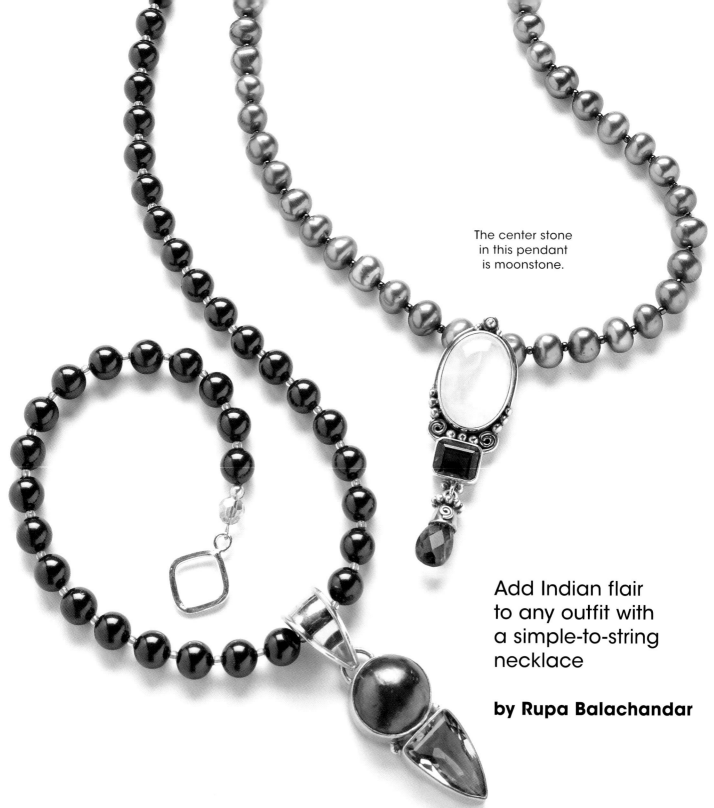

The center stone
in this pendant
is moonstone.

Add Indian flair
to any outfit with
a simple-to-string
necklace

by Rupa Balachandar

String exotic
elegance

A single strand of pearls and a gemstone-studded pendant look lovely against a bright sari or summery tank top. I chose bold hues that remind me of my home country, but you can use a neutral palette for a more subtle statement. Either way, this necklace gives you a taste of India without too much Bollywood bling.

1 necklace • Cut a piece of beading wire (Basics, p. 12). Center a pendant.

2 On each end, string an alternating pattern of a pearl and an 11º seed bead until the strand is within 1½ in. (3.8 cm) of the finished length.

3 On each end, string a crimp bead and a 4–6 mm bead. Attach half of a clasp (Basics).

1 earrings • Cut a 3-in. (7.6 cm) piece of wire. String a briolette and make a set of wraps above it (Basics).

2 String a cone and an 11º seed bead. Make a wrapped loop (Basics).

3 Open the loop of a decorative earring wire (Basics). Attach the dangle and close the loop. Make a second earring.

Supplies

necklace 16 in. (41 cm)
- 50–60 mm multistone pendant
- 16-in. (41 cm) strand 7–8 mm pearls
- **2** 4–6 mm beads
- 1 g 11º seed beads
- flexible beading wire, .014 or .015
- **2** crimp beads
- box or toggle clasp
- chainnose or crimping pliers
- diagonal wire cutters

earrings
- **2** 12–13 mm briolettes
- **2** 11º seed beads
- 6 in. (15 cm) 24-gauge wire
- **2** 12–13 mm cones
- pair of decorative earring wires
- chainnose and roundnose pliers
- diagonal wire cutters

Tip

If your pearls won't fit through the bail of the pendant, string a few seed beads at the center of the wire.

Ojime and pearls

Bring together a novelty focal bead and classic pearls for a fanciful yet wearable set

by Irina Miech

❝This piece was inspired by an octopus I saw while snorkeling in Tahiti.❞ —IM

These wooden beads are called ojime (pronounced oh-jeem-eh). They are made from boxwood using traditional Japanese patterns. Details like hand-carved scales and tiny onyx eyes add to their charm. Make a sea-inspired lariat with a whimsical swimmer followed by a playful trail of pearl bubbles. A single strand of diagonally drilled pearls is enough to make a lariat and earrings.

1 lariat · On a head pin, string an 8–12 mm pearl and make a wrapped loop (Basics, p. 12). Make two pearl units. Set aside for step 7.

2 Cut a 6-ft. (1.8 m) piece of beading wire. String 1½ in. (3.8 cm) of three 11º or 13º seed beads alternated with 4–5 mm pearls. Center the beads.

3 Over both ends, string an ojime focal bead.

4 On each end, string 14½ in. (36.8 cm) of seed beads.

5 On one end, string a 6 mm pearl and 1¼ in. (3.2 cm) of seed beads. Continue stringing 6 mms alternated with segments of seed beads for 12 in. (30 cm). In each segment, decrease the number of seed beads. End with one seed bead.

6 On the other end, string 1½ in. (3.8 cm) of seed beads. String 6 mm pearls alternated with segments of seed beads as in step 5.

7 On each end, string eight 6 mm pearls, a crimp bead, and a pearl unit. Check the fit; one end should be about 1½ in. (3.8 cm) longer than the other. Add or remove beads if necessary. Go back through the crimp bead and tighten the wire. Crimp the crimp bead (Basics) and trim the excess wire.

Supplies

lariat 64 in. (1.6 m)
- 15–25 mm ojime focal bead
- **2** 8–12 mm pearls
- 16-in. (41 cm) strand 6 mm pearls, diagonally drilled
- **7-9** 4-5 mm pearls
- 15 g 11º or 13º seed beads
- flexible beading wire, .014 or .015
- **2** 1½-in. (3.8 cm) head pins
- **2** crimp beads
- chainnose and roundnose pliers
- diagonal wire cutters
- crimping pliers (optional)

earrings
- **2** 8–12 mm pearls
- **16** 6 mm pearls, diagonally drilled
- 8 in. (20 cm) 24-gauge half-hard wire
- **2** 1½-in. (3.8 cm) head pins
- pair of earring wires
- chainnose and roundnose pliers
- diagonal wire cutters

1 earrings • Follow step 1 of the lariat to make a pearl unit.
Cut a 4-in. (10 cm) piece of wire. Make the first half of a wrapped loop (Basics) on one end. Attach the pearl unit and complete the wraps.

2 String eight 6 mm pearls and make a wrapped loop.

3 Open the loop of an earring wire (Basics). Attach the dangle and close the loop. Make a second earring.

Tip

If you use .014 or .015 beading wire, you probably won't be able to go back through the pearls when finishing. If this is a concern, consider using thinner beading wire, such as .012, or use an additional crimp bead on each end.

Design alternative

To make a thicker lariat, substitute larger beads and string a larger loop in steps 2 and 3. This version uses diagonally drilled stick pearls, and small pearls replace the seed beads.

Mix a glass menagerie

Combining glass "species" creates a harmonious whole

by Cathy Jakicic

Putting lampworked glass beads next to rough, recycled-glass nuggets may not be the obvious choice, but they share a remarkable luminescence. Accented with Czech beads, sea-glass style beads, and bicone crystals, they are a clearly beautiful arrangement.

Supplies

necklace 20 in. (51 cm)
- **5** 20 mm lampworked lentil beads
- **3** 18–29 mm (medium) river rock recycled-glass beads
- **6** 15–18 mm sea-glass style beads
- **4** 11 mm lampworked rondelles
- **18–24** 10 mm faceted Czech glass rondelles
- **26–36** 4 mm bicone crystals
- flexible beading wire, .014 or .015
- **4** crimp beads
- 34 mm toggle clasp
- chainnose or crimping pliers
- diagonal wire cutters

earrings
- **2** 11 mm lampworked rondelles
- **2** 6 mm crystal rondelles
- **2** 4 mm bicone crystals
- 2 in. (5 cm) chain, 5–6 mm links
- **2** 2-in. (5 cm) head pins
- pair of long earring wires
- chainnose and roundnose pliers
- diagonal wire cutters

Technique: Clasp

When attaching the clasp (Basics, p. 12), add extra bicones to the bar end so the clasp doesn't cover any of the focal beads.

❝The violet and gold combination is my favorite palette for the transition between winter and spring.**❞** —CJ

3

String an alternating pattern of bicones and Czech glass rondelles until the strand is within 6 in. (15 cm) of the finished length.

Tip

Plan the necklace on a bead board and position the clasp exactly where you want it.

2

String about 5 in. (13 cm) of sea-glass style beads, lampworked rondelles, Czech glass rondelles, and bicones.

String about 5 in. (13 cm) of lampworked beads, river rock beads, and bicones. Attach a toggle clasp (Technique, p. 197).

4

1

necklace • Cut a piece of beading wire (Basics). String about 4 in. (10 cm) of lampworked beads, river rock beads, and bicone crystals.

1 earrings • For each earring: On a head pin, string a bicone crystal, a lampworked rondelle, and a crystal rondelle. Make the first half of a wrapped loop (Basics).

2 Cut two links of chain. Attach the bead unit to the chain and complete the wraps. Attach the dangle to the earring wire, pinching the loop closed.

Color note

The bicone crystals are cyclamen opal, the sea-glass style beads are amethyst, and the river rock beads are peach pink.

Design alternative

Bring the river rock nuggets to the forefront for a more budget-friendly — but still glowing — necklace.

Mixed

media

Ruffle
necklace

Transform fabric scraps into a crafty centerpiece

by Rebekah Gough

Making a ruffle necklace is a fun and
trendy way to use up extra fabric, beads,
or buttons you have on hand. I attached
chain on this necklace but ribbon
is another stylish option.

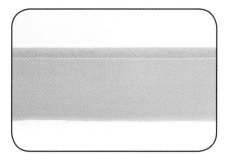

1 Fold a piece of fabric in half and iron it. About ¼ in. (6 mm) from the fold, sew a straight seam to create a sleeve for the wire.

2 Cut an 8-in. (20 cm) piece of wire. Make a wrapped loop (Basics) larger than the opening of the sleeve. Pull the sleeve over the wire and make a large wrapped loop.

3 About 1 in. (2.5 cm) from one side, sew a button to the ruffle.

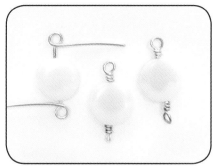

4 Cut a 3-in. (7.6 cm) piece of wire. Make the first half of a wrapped loop (Basics). String a bead and make the first half of a wrapped loop. Make six bead units. Complete the wraps on four units.

5 To make a bead connector: On each side of an unwrapped bead unit, attach a wrapped loop unit. Complete the wraps. Make two connectors.

6 On each side, open a jump ring (Basics) and attach a loop of the fabric pendant and a loop of a bead connector. Close the jump ring.

7 Cut a 7–9-in. (18–23 cm) piece of chain. Cut the chain in half. On each side, use a jump ring to connect a chain and a bead connector.

8 Check the fit, and trim chain if necessary. Use a jump ring to attach a lobster claw clasp to one end. Attach a jump ring to the other end.

"I made some cute ruffle curtains for my kitchen and decided I needed one for my neck." –RG

Supplies

necklace 18 in. (46 cm)

- **6** 12 mm beads
- 26–30 mm button
- 3 x 18 in. (7.6 x 46 cm) fabric
- 26 in. (66 cm) 20-gauge half-hard wire
- 7–9 in. (18–23 cm) chain, 3–4 mm links
- **6** 5 mm jump rings
- lobster claw clasp
- chainnose and roundnose pliers
- diagonal wire cutters
- iron and ironing board
- needle and thread
- scissors
- sewing machine

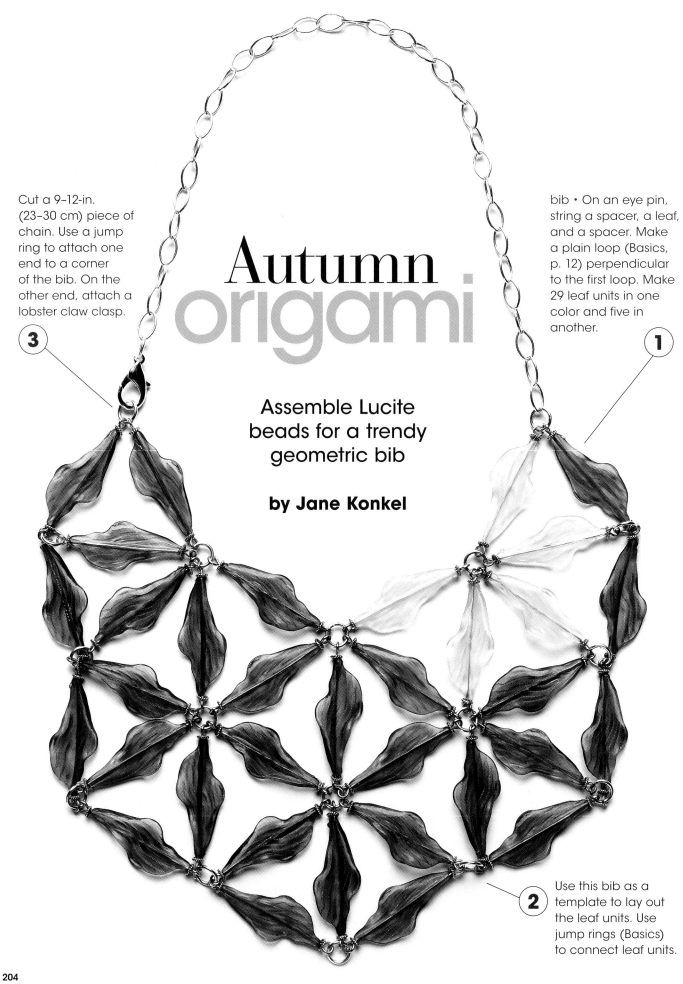

Autumn
origami

Assemble Lucite
beads for a trendy
geometric bib

by Jane Konkel

3 Cut a 9–12-in.
(23–30 cm) piece of
chain. Use a jump
ring to attach one
end to a corner
of the bib. On the
other end, attach a
lobster claw clasp.

1 bib • On an eye pin,
string a spacer, a leaf,
and a spacer. Make
a plain loop (Basics,
p. 12) perpendicular
to the first loop. Make
29 leaf units in one
color and five in
another.

2 Use this bib as a
template to lay out
the leaf units. Use
jump rings (Basics)
to connect leaf units.

dangle earrings • For each earring: Make a leaf unit. Attach a top-drilled leaf to one loop and an earring wire to the other loop.

hoop earrings • For each earring: String beads, spacers, and a top-drilled leaf as desired. Using chainnose pliers, make a bend ¼ in. (6 mm) from the end.

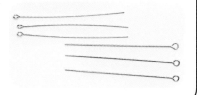

Tip

If you're looking for a frugal option, you can save a few bucks by using base metal eye pins instead of sterling silver.

Design alternative

The pattern for this necklace will work with other beads, as long as the beads are narrow and of the same length. Here's an option I strung with twisted wood beads.

Supplies

necklace 28 in. (71 cm)
- **34** 32 mm Lucite twisted leaves, **29** in one color, **5** in another
- **68** 3 mm flat spacers
- 9–12 in. (23–30 cm) chain, 7–9 mm links
- **34** 2-in. (5 cm) 20-gauge eye pins
- **17** 7 mm jump rings
- 4 mm jump ring
- lobster claw clasp
- chainnose and roundnose pliers
- diagonal wire cutters

dangle earrings
- **2** 32 mm Lucite twisted leaves
- **2** 16 mm Lucite beech leaves, top-drilled

- **4** 4 mm flat spacers
- **2** 2-in. (5 cm) 20-gauge eye pins
- pair of earring wires
- chainnose and roundnose pliers
- diagonal wire cutters

hoop earrings
- **2** 16 mm Lucite beech leaves, top-drilled
- **8** 6 mm Lucite round beads
- **12** 4 mm flat spacers
- pair of earring hoops
- chainnose pliers

Give your set a factory feel with oxidized chain and a hammered metal ring. Use different finishes and crystal colors for a unique look.

Nature & industry joined by design

A few simple components can bring together divergent themes

by Catherine Hodge

Before making this set, I spent time just thinking about where I live; I actually listed what Michigan means to me. Natural elements, like the beach, woods, birds, and snow, as well as industrial aspects, like old buildings, cars, and factories, kept appearing on my list. Looking through my bead stash, I found goodies relating to the two themes.

1 necklace • Cut a 3-in. (7.6 cm) piece of 24-gauge wire. String a briolette and make a set of wraps above it (Basics, p. 12). Make the first half of a wrapped loop (Basics) perpendicular to the bead.

2 Cut a 2-in. (5 cm) piece of 24-gauge wire. Make the first half of a wrapped loop. String a bicone crystal and make the first half of a wrapped loop perpendicular to the first. Make seven bicone units. Using 20-gauge wire, make a bicone unit with a 7 mm loop.

Supplies

necklace 19 in. (48 cm)
- ◆ 8–12 mm briolette
- ◆ **8** 4 mm bicone crystals
- ◆ 32 mm square rod drop
- ◆ 10–18 mm charm with two holes
- ◆ **3** 5–20 mm charms
- ◆ 24 mm hammered ring
- ◆ 2 in. (5 cm) 20-gauge wire
- ◆ 17 in. (43 cm) 24-gauge wire
- ◆ 16–20 in. (41–51 cm) chain, 3–5 mm links
- ◆ **5** 5–6 mm jump rings
- ◆ lobster claw clasp
- ◆ chainnose and roundnose pliers
- ◆ diagonal wire cutters

earrings
- ◆ **2** 8–12 mm briolettes
- ◆ **2** 32 mm square rod drops
- ◆ **2** 7 mm charms
- ◆ 6 in. (15 cm) 24-gauge wire
- ◆ 3 in. (7.6 cm) chain, 3–5 mm links
- ◆ **2** 4 mm jump rings
- ◆ pair of earring wires
- ◆ chainnose and roundnose pliers
- ◆ diagonal wire cutters

3 Attach one loop of a 24-gauge bicone unit to a hammered ring. Cut two ¾-in. (1.9 cm) pieces of chain. Connect the other loop to a chain. Complete the wraps. Repeat on the other side of the ring.

4 Cut two 2-in. (5 cm) and two 5–7-in. (13–18 cm) pieces of chain. On each side, attach: bicone unit, 2-in. (5 cm) chain, bicone unit, 5–7-in. (13–18 cm) chain. Complete the wraps as you go.

5 On one end, use a bicone unit to attach a lobster claw clasp. On the other end, attach the 20-gauge bicone unit.

Tip

In step 5, you can use a bicone unit to attach a soldered jump ring instead of making a bead unit with a large loop in step 2.

6 Attach the briolette unit and the bottom hole of a charm. Complete the wraps. Open a jump ring (Basics) and attach the dangle to the hammered ring. Close the jump ring.

7 Use jump rings to attach the remaining charms to the ring.

1 earrings • Follow necklace step 1 to make a briolette unit. Attach it to a 1½-in. (3.8 cm) piece of chain and complete the wraps.

2 Open the loop of an earring wire (Basics). Attach a bird charm and a square rod drop. Close the loop.

3 Open a jump ring (Basics). Attach the chain and the loop of the earring wire. Close the jump ring. Make a second earring.

"Currently my biggest challenge is having too many supplies. Sometimes I'm overwhelmed by the options, and I get distracted by sorting and putting things away instead of creating." —CH

Tip

You can buy gunmetal chain, or to get an industrial look like the necklace on page 206, use liver of sulfur to add a patina to metal.

A new angle on
dangles

Forget head pins — beading wire is the stuff these earrings are made of ◆ **by Carolina Angel**

Designing jewelry is about embracing challenges. So, when life handed me beading wire instead of head pins, I still made earrings! A stack of metallic beads nicely disguises the wire that loops through a briolette at the bottom of the dangle. The resulting earring is as flexible as the design possibilities.

Supplies

- **2** 10–20 mm gemstone briolettes
- stardust beads
  - **2** 7 mm rounds
  - **8** 4 mm rondelles
  - **6** 4 mm rounds
  - **6** 3 mm rondelles
  - **2** 3 mm rounds
- **2** 3 mm bicone crystals
- flexible beading wire, .010
- **2** crimp beads
- pair of earring wires
- chainnose or crimping pliers
- diagonal wire cutters

1 Cut a 9-in. (23 cm) piece of beading wire and center a briolette. On each end, string a 3 mm rondelle, a 4 mm round, and a 4 mm rondelle.

2 Over both ends, string a 7 mm round, a 4 mm round, a 3 mm rondelle, and two 4 mm rondelles.

Design alternative

No beading wire? No problem! I made this pair of earrings with white nylon thread. Simply tie a knot (Basics) instead of using a crimp bead.

3 Over both ends, string a crimp bead, a 3 mm round, a bicone crystal, and the loop of an earring wire. Go back through the last few beads strung and tighten the wires. Crimp the crimp bead (Basics, p. 12) and trim the excess wire. Make a second earring.

Tip

For this project, use .010 beading wire, since four strands of wire must pass through the top beads.

Twice as nice

Chain and silk ribbon make a bright, textured backdrop for whimsical charms. Wear this piece as a simple necklace or wrap it several times for a colorful cuff. Complete the look with mismatched earrings using crystals that coordinate with the ribbon's color.

1 necklace/bracelet • Open a jump ring (Basics, p. 12). Attach a charm. Close the jump ring. Attach jump rings to seven charms.

2 Cut a 36–38-in. (91–97 cm) piece of chain and a 5-in. (13 cm) piece of wire. About 2 in. (5 cm) from one end of the chain, and about 4 in. (10 cm) from one end of the ribbon, string the wire through a link and wrap the wire a few times around the ribbon. Trim the excess wire and tuck the end under the wraps.

3 At 5–7-in. (13–18 cm) intervals, use wire to attach the chain and ribbon as in step 2. Do not trim the excess chain.

4 Use a jump ring to attach five charm units as desired. Attach the charm units either to the chain or to the ribbon.

5 Over both ribbon ends, string a large-hole bead. On each end, string a charm unit and tie an overhand knot (Basics).

> **"I love to work with everything colorful and any fiber."**
> —UB

Wire-wrap chain and ribbon for a versatile necklace or bracelet

by Ute Bernsen

For a bold cuff, attach large Lucite flowers and vintage charms.

1 earrings • On a head pin, string a crystal. Make a plain loop (Basics). Repeat.

2 Cut a ¾-in. (1.9 cm) piece of chain. Open a jump ring (Basics) and attach a charm and one end of the chain. Close the jump ring.

3 Open the loop of an earring wire (Basics) and attach the chain. Close the loop.

4 Open the loop of each crystal unit and attach the chain. Close the loop. Make a second earring.

Tips

• If you make a necklace with antique brass chain, you can use 24-gauge Artistic Wire to match. The "gunmetal" color is actually more of an antique brass.

• If you're having trouble stringing the ribbons through the hole of a bead, use a straightened paper clip to push the ends through.

Supplies

necklace/bracelet 41 in. (1 m)
- **7** 9–25 mm charms
- 7–9 mm large-hole bead
- 40–42 in. (1–1.1 m) ribbon, 15 mm width
- 30 in. (76 cm) 24-gauge wire
- 36–38 in. (91–97 cm) chain, 3–4 mm links
- **12** 4–5 mm jump rings
- chainnose and roundnose pliers, or **2** pairs of chainnose pliers
- diagonal wire cutters

earrings
- **2** 9–25 mm charms
- **4** 5–6 mm crystals
- 2 in. (5 cm) chain, 3–4 mm links
- **4** 1½-in. (3.8 cm) head pins
- **2** 4–5 mm jump rings
- pair of earring wires
- chainnose and roundnose pliers
- diagonal wire cutters

A new *slant* on bails

Give weight to a necklace
with an alternative use
for pendant bails

by Mary Champion

Chips are an
economical
choice for this
necklace.

On a trip to Santa Fe, N.M., I went to see the artists and art that the city is famous for. I absolutely fell in love with the Native American jewelry so, when I came home, I just had to do something with my inspiration. I started making necklaces, bracelets, and earrings using materials (like pendant bails) in unique ways. Another source of my inspiration comes from my childhood memories of the ocean, as in this mother-of-pearl necklace and the watery blue color of the lace agate version.

1 necklace • Cut a 6-in. (15 cm) piece of 20-gauge wire. On one end, make a plain loop (Basics, p. 12). String: 5 mm spacer, oval bead, bail, oval, bail, oval, bail, oval. Make a plain loop.

2 Close a crimp cover over the bottom loop.

3 Cut three 12-in. (30 cm) pieces of beading wire. On each wire, string a crimp bead and the top loop. Go back through the crimp bead and tighten the wire. Crimp the crimp bead (Basics).

4 Over all three wires, string a large-hole spacer. On each wire, string 7–8 in. (18–20 cm) of 11º seed beads.

5 Cut a 14-in. (36 cm) piece of beading wire. String a crimp bead and the loop of a bail. Go back through the crimp bead and tighten the wire. Crimp the crimp bead. Close a crimp cover over the crimp. String 3–4 in. (7.6–10 cm) of chips.

6 **a** String a 3–4 mm spacer and 4–5 in. (10–13 cm) of 11ºs.
b Repeat steps 5 and 6a with the remaining bails.

7 On each side, on each wire, string a crimp bead and a loop of half of a clasp. Check the fit, and add or remove beads if necessary. Go back through the last few beads strung and tighten the wire. Crimp the crimp bead and trim the excess wire.

8 Close a crimp cover over each crimp.

Supplies

necklace 20 in. (51 cm)

- ◆ **4** 18 mm oval beads
- ◆ 16-in. (41 cm) strand 6–10 mm chips
- ◆ **8 g** 11º seed beads
- ◆ 6–9 mm large-hole spacer
- ◆ 5 mm spacer
- ◆ **3** 3–4 mm round spacers
- ◆ **3** 6 mm bails
- ◆ flexible beading wire, .014 or .015
- ◆ 6 in. (15 cm) 20-gauge half-hard wire
- ◆ **12** crimp beads
- ◆ **10** crimp covers
- ◆ three-strand clasp
- ◆ chainnose and roundnose pliers
- ◆ diagonal wire cutters
- ◆ crimping pliers (optional)

earrings

- ◆ **2** 18 mm oval beads
- ◆ **36–40** 6–10 mm chips
- ◆ **2 g** 11º seed beads
- ◆ **2** 5 mm spacers
- ◆ flexible beading wire, .014 or .015
- ◆ **2** three-to-one connectors
- ◆ **2** 2-in. (5 cm) head pins
- ◆ **4** crimp beads
- ◆ **6** crimp covers
- ◆ pair of earring wires
- ◆ chainnose and roundnose pliers
- ◆ diagonal wire cutters
- ◆ crimping pliers (optional)

1 earrings • On a head pin, string an 11º seed bead, a spacer, an oval bead, and an 11º. Make a plain loop (Basics).

3 Cut a 6-in. (15 cm) piece of beading wire. String a crimp bead and an outer loop of the connector. Go back through the crimp bead and tighten the wire. Crimp the crimp bead (Basics).

5 Close a crimp cover over each crimp. Open the loop of an earring wire. Attach the dangle and close the loop. Make a second earring to match the first.

Tip

For added dimension, use a large crimp cover in step 3 of the necklace.

2 Open the loop (Basics) and attach the middle loop of a three-to-one connector. Close the loop. Close a crimp cover over the top 11º.

4 String 3 in. (7.6 cm) of 11ºs and chips. String a crimp bead and the connector's remaining loop. Go back through the last few beads strung and tighten the wire. Crimp the crimp bead and trim the excess wire.

Design alternative

Sometimes a fancy necklace calls for the simplest earrings. Use a few leftover beads to make an easy pair of drops.

Remembering Rusland

String a trans-Siberian set ◆ by Stacy Werkheiser

When you think of Russia, you may envision nesting Matryoshka dolls or the carnival-colored domes of St. Basil's Cathedral. I see Saint George (the patron saint of Moscow) slaying a dragon, clusters of pastel summer cottages called *dachas*, and traditional hand-painted lacquer boxes lining the stalls of local flea markets. This oval focal bead echoes Russian box motifs in miniature. It has comrades in a range of palettes and designs, representing the many facets of this colorful country.

1 necklace • On a head pin, string a 3 mm spacer, a 4 mm spacer, and an oval bead. Make a wrapped loop (Basics, p. 12). Trim the head from a head pin. Make the first half of a wrapped loop and attach the oval-bead unit. Complete the wraps. String a 6 mm bead and make a wrapped loop.

2 Cut a piece of beading wire (Basics). Center the pendant. On each side, string a 3 mm, an 8 mm bead, a 4 mm, and an 8 mm crystal.

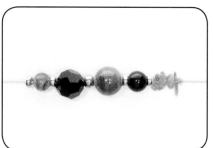

3 On each end, string: 3 mm, 5 mm bead, 3 mm, crystal, 4 mm, 8 mm bead, 3 mm, 6 mm bead, 3 mm, five chips. Repeat until the strand is within 1½ in. (3.8 cm) of the finished length.

4 On each end, string a 6 mm bead, a crimp bead, and a 5 mm bead. Attach half of a box clasp (Basics). Close a crimp cover over each crimp if desired.

1 bracelet • Cut three pieces of beading wire (Basics). On each of two (outer) wires, string: 6 mm bead, 5 mm bead, spacer, 5 mm, 6 mm, spacer, 8 mm bead, spacer, 8 mm crystal, spacer.

2a On each of the two wires, string: 5 mm, 6 mm, spacer, 6 mm, 5 mm, spacer, crystal, spacer, 8 mm bead, spacer.

b Repeat the patterns from steps 1 and 2a until the strands are within 1½ in. (3.8 cm) of the finished length.

3 On the remaining (middle) wire, string: 8 mm bead, spacer, 6 mm, 5 mm, spacer, crystal, spacer, 8 mm bead, spacer.

5 On each end of each strand, string a crimp bead and a 5 mm. Attach the corresponding loop of half of a box clasp (Basics). Close a crimp cover over each crimp if desired.

4 String the pattern from steps 1 and 2a, then string: 6 mm, 5 mm, spacer, crystal.

" I had no trouble choosing a palette: To me, the people, culture, and history of Russia are painted in cool tones. But there's a long tradition of riches and royalty, too, so I used gold accents.**"**
–SW

Supplies

necklace 16 in. (41 cm)

- 25 mm oval painted bead (Artbeads.com)
- **10–12** 8 mm round crystals
- **10–12** 8 mm round beads
- **9–11** 6 mm round beads
- **10–12** 5 mm round beads, in same color as 8 mm round beads
- **30–40** 3–6 mm gemstone chips
- **11–13** 4 mm spacers
- **33–41** 3 mm spacers
- flexible beading wire, .014 or .015
- **2** 2-in. (5 cm) head pins
- **2** crimp beads
- **2** crimp covers (optional)
- box clasp
- chainnose and roundnose pliers
- diagonal wire cutters
- crimping pliers (optional)

bracelet

- **10–13** 8 mm round crystals
- **10–13** 8 mm round beads
- **22–28** 6 mm round beads
- **28–31** 5 mm round beads, in same color as 8 mm round beads
- **39–45** 4 mm spacers
- flexible beading wire, .014 or .015
- **6** crimp beads
- **6** crimp covers (optional)
- three-strand box clasp
- chainnose or crimping pliers
- diagonal wire cutters

Short and chic

Adjust the length of the earrings by adding or removing jump rings.

Linked jump rings are perfect for dainty dangles

by Susan Kennedy

I love dangle earrings, but I don't like anything too heavy or long. Brass-colored jump rings, lampworked beads, and some tiny accents add up to a perfect pair.

1 Open a 7 mm jump ring (Basics, p. 12). Attach a drop and close the jump ring. Use a 10 mm jump ring to attach a lampworked bead and the drop unit.

2 On a head pin, string a rondelle. Make a wrapped loop (Basics).

Supplies

- ◆ **2** 12 mm round large-hole lampworked beads
- ◆ **2** 6 mm rondelles
- ◆ **2** 6 mm drops
- ◆ **2** 1½-in. (3.8 cm) head pins
- ◆ **2** 10 mm jump rings
- ◆ **4** 7 mm jump rings
- ◆ **2** 5 mm jump rings
- ◆ pair of earring wires
- ◆ chainnose and roundnose pliers
- ◆ diagonal wire cutters

3 Use a 7 mm jump ring to attach the rondelle unit to the drop unit.

4 Use a 5 mm jump ring to attach the rondelle unit to an earring wire. Make a second earring the mirror image of the first.

Embroidered
details

**Combine lace
doilies and
embroidery floss
in crafty hoop
earrings**

by Sonia Kumar

Here's a chance to turn vintage doilies into wearable heirlooms: Stitch them to hoops with embroidery floss. Use whatever size floss you like (the higher the number, the thinner the thread) but remember that with thinner floss you may need to go around the hoop a second time to cover it completely. Because embroidery floss is available in hundreds of colors, you'll be able to create many beautiful pairings.

1 Cut a circle about 1½ in. (3.8 cm) in diameter from the center of a doily.

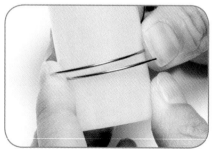

2 Cut a 5–7-in. (13–18 cm) piece of 18-gauge wire. Wrap it around a film canister or aspirin bottle to make a hoop the same size as the doily. The ends should overlap by about ¼ in. (6 mm). Trim the excess wire.

3 Cut a 3-in. (7.6 cm) piece of 28-gauge wire and wrap it tightly around the overlapping ends. Trim the excess wire.

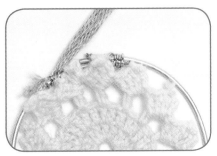

4 Cut a 5-ft. (1.5 m) piece of embroidery floss. String a needle, centering it on the floss.

Cut a 2-in. (5 cm) piece of 28-gauge wire. Wrap the wire tightly around the hoop and the ends of the floss to tack it down.

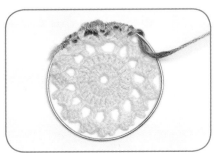

5 String the needle through and around the doily's edges, wrapping the floss around the hoop to attach the doily.

6 If desired, wrap the floss around the hoop a second time.

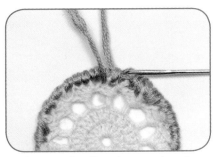

7 Secure the floss by passing the needle under the previous wraps. Trim the excess.

8 Cut a 14-in. (36 cm) piece of 28-gauge wire. Wrap it around the hoop tightly. Just before you've wrapped the entire hoop, wrap the wire through a soldered jump ring to attach it to the hoop. Trim the excess wire.

9 Open the loop of an earring wire (Basics, p. 12). Attach the jump ring and close the loop. Make a second earring.

Supplies

- **2** lace doilies
- 10 ft. (3 m) embroidery floss
- 10–14 in. (25–36 cm) 18-gauge copper wire
- 38 in. (97 cm) 28-gauge wire
- **2** 6–8 mm soldered jump rings
- pair of earring wires
- chainnose and roundnose pliers
- diagonal wire cutters
- embroidery needle (or sewing needle with large eye)
- 35 mm film canister or aspirin bottle

Design alternative

If you prefer to skip the lace, you can still wrap embroidery floss to make colorful hoops. I attached pearls so the earrings had some movement. (Use the largest part of your roundnose pliers to make the loops of the bead units.)

Tip

You won't need quite as much wire as I called for, but I found that it's easier to pull wire tightly when the end is a bit longer. The same goes for the embroidery floss: Because it's inexpensive, I prefer to have excess while I'm attaching the doily.

Shades of
light and dark

**Forest and front yard meet in an eclectic
necklace and earrings ◆ by Jean Yates**

In the 1700s, farmers cleared and plowed the rocky soil in Pound
Ridge, N.Y., where I live. Now I see the stone walls they built
crumbling and covered with fallen trees. It's odd to think that the
woods have once again taken over the carefully tilled farmland.
This necklace reflects the eerie feeling I get when I step from the
sunlight of my landscaped front yard and am instantly engulfed
by the shadows and coolness of the overgrown forest. I chose the
pendant to show how I envision the wildness and beauty so close
to my yard; it reflects that sense of timelessness.

66Since 1977, my
family and I have
lived only minutes
from New York
City. The area is
a fascinating tangle
of dark woods
and brilliant
sunshine.99 –JY

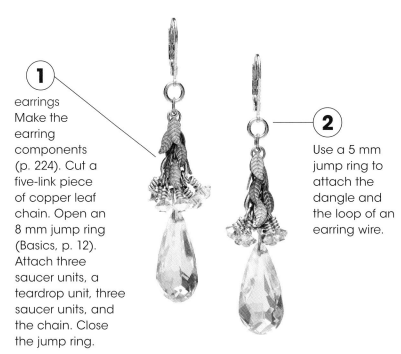

1 earrings
Make the
earring
components
(p. 224). Cut a
five-link piece
of copper leaf
chain. Open an
8 mm jump ring
(Basics, p. 12).
Attach three
saucer units, a
teardrop unit, three
saucer units, and
the chain. Close
the jump ring.

2 Use a 5 mm
jump ring to
attach the
dangle and
the loop of an
earring wire.

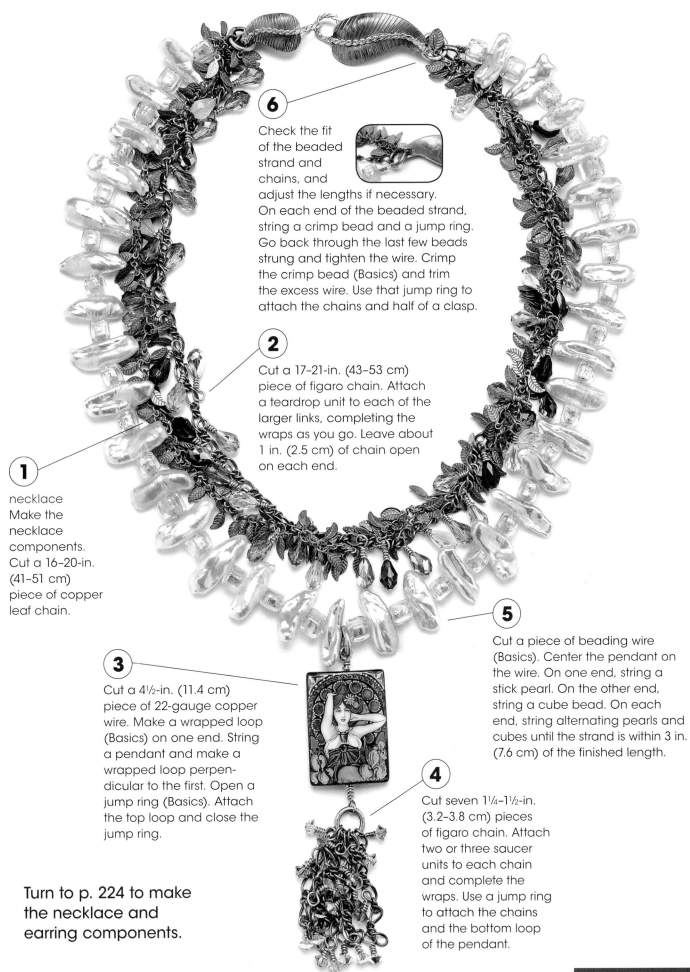

6

Check the fit of the beaded strand and chains, and adjust the lengths if necessary. On each end of the beaded strand, string a crimp bead and a jump ring. Go back through the last few beads strung and tighten the wire. Crimp the crimp bead (Basics) and trim the excess wire. Use that jump ring to attach the chains and half of a clasp.

2

Cut a 17–21-in. (43–53 cm) piece of figaro chain. Attach a teardrop unit to each of the larger links, completing the wraps as you go. Leave about 1 in. (2.5 cm) of chain open on each end.

1

necklace
Make the necklace components. Cut a 16–20-in. (41–51 cm) piece of copper leaf chain.

3

Cut a 4½-in. (11.4 cm) piece of 22-gauge copper wire. Make a wrapped loop (Basics) on one end. String a pendant and make a wrapped loop perpendicular to the first. Open a jump ring (Basics). Attach the top loop and close the jump ring.

5

Cut a piece of beading wire (Basics). Center the pendant on the wire. On one end, string a stick pearl. On the other end, string a cube bead. On each end, string alternating pearls and cubes until the strand is within 3 in. (7.6 cm) of the finished length.

4

Cut seven 1¼–1½-in. (3.2–3.8 cm) pieces of figaro chain. Attach two or three saucer units to each chain and complete the wraps. Use a jump ring to attach the chains and the bottom loop of the pendant.

Turn to p. 224 to make the necklace and earring components.

Earring components

teardrop unit • Cut a 1½-in. (3.8 cm) piece of 24-gauge copper wire. Center a 24 mm teardrop pendant. Bend the wire up around the teardrop. With each end, make a loop perpendicular to the teardrop. Wrap the ends around the wire stem and trim the excess wire. Make two teardrop units.

saucer unit • On a head pin, string a saucer crystal. Make a wrapped loop (Basics). Make 12 saucer units.

Necklace components

teardrop unit • On a head pin, string a 9 mm teardrop crystal. Make the first half of a wrapped loop (Basics). Make 44 to 52 teardrop units.

saucer unit • On a head pin, string a saucer crystal. Make the first half of a wrapped loop. Make 18 to 22 saucer units.

This pendant is enameled and coated with antitarnish lacquer.

Brass *and* blue

A hand-crafted pendant is the focal point of a stunning set

by **Helene Tsigistras**

I bought the supplies for these projects at the 2008 Bead&Button Show and later learned that the pendant was made in a South African village by local craftspeople employed by Metalcraft by DeZine. Brass paired with turquoise blue is a beautiful combination that always seems to be in season.

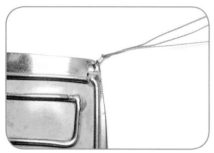

1 **necklace** • Cut three pieces of beading wire (Basics, p. 12). Cut the wires in half. Over three wires, string a crimp bead and a hole of the pendant. Go back through the crimp bead and tighten the wires. Crimp the crimp bead (Basics). Repeat on the other side of the pendant.

2 On each side, over two wires, string a tube bead. Separate the wires. On one wire, string coins; on the other, string tubes until the strands are within 2 in. (5 cm) of the finished length.

3 On each of the remaining wires, string 5 mm rounds until the strands are within 2 in. (5 cm) of the finished length.

4 On each end, over all three wires, string a cone and a 6 mm spacer, and attach a clasp (Basics).

Supplies

necklace 21 in. (53 cm)
- 50 mm pendant, with 2 holes
- 16-in. (41 cm) strand 13 mm tube beads
- 16-in. (41 cm) strand 12 mm lava rock coins
- 16-in. (41 cm) strand 5 mm round beads
- **2** 6 mm spacers
- flexible beading wire, .014 or .015
- **2** cones
- **4** crimp beads
- **2** hook clasps
- chainnose or crimping pliers
- diagonal wire cutters

earrings
- **2** 13 mm tube beads
- **2** 5 mm round beads
- **2** 1½-in. (3.8 cm) head pins
- pair of earring wires
- chainnose and roundnose pliers
- diagonal wire cutters

"I am drawn to blues and greens and earth tones. I like crystals, natural gemstones, and unusual shapes and textures, as well as metal elements." —HT

1 earrings • On a head pin, string a 5 mm bead and a tube. Make a wrapped loop (Basics).

2 Open the loop of an earring wire (Basics). Attach the dangle and close the loop. Make a second earring to match the first.

Tips

• If you like the look of a twisted necklace, loosely braid the strands before stringing the cones.

• Rather than cutting heavy chain (pictured at right), use heavy-duty pliers to open and close the links.

Design alternative

For a simplified version, attach a pendant to heavy chain with large jump rings.

Softer side of
stringing

I'm always looking for ways to add something unexpected to a design. When I can remove a bit of expense at the same time, all the better. I used silk ribbon instead of chain to finish off this simple gemstone-and-silver strand. I didn't scrimp on the silver beads and cones, so it was nice to save money with the silk while adding a beautiful splash of color and elegant drape.

1 necklace • Cut a 3-in. (7.6 cm) piece of 20-gauge wire. Make a wrapped loop (Basics, p. 12) on each end. Make two connectors. Set aside for step 4.

2 Cut a 14-in. (36 cm) piece of beading wire. On the wire, center an alternating pattern of three beads and two flat spacers. If your beads are different sizes, use larger ones in the center.

3 On each side, string about 3 in. (7.6 cm) of beads in an alternating pattern.

4 On each end, string two beads, a crimp bead, and one loop of a connector. Go back through the beads just strung and tighten the wire. Crimp the crimp bead (Basics) and trim the excess wire. On each end, center a ribbon on the remaining loop.

5 On each side, over both ends of the ribbon, string a cone. To wear, tie the ends together.

Tip

For easier stringing, use a folded piece of flexible beading wire to draw the ribbon through the cone.

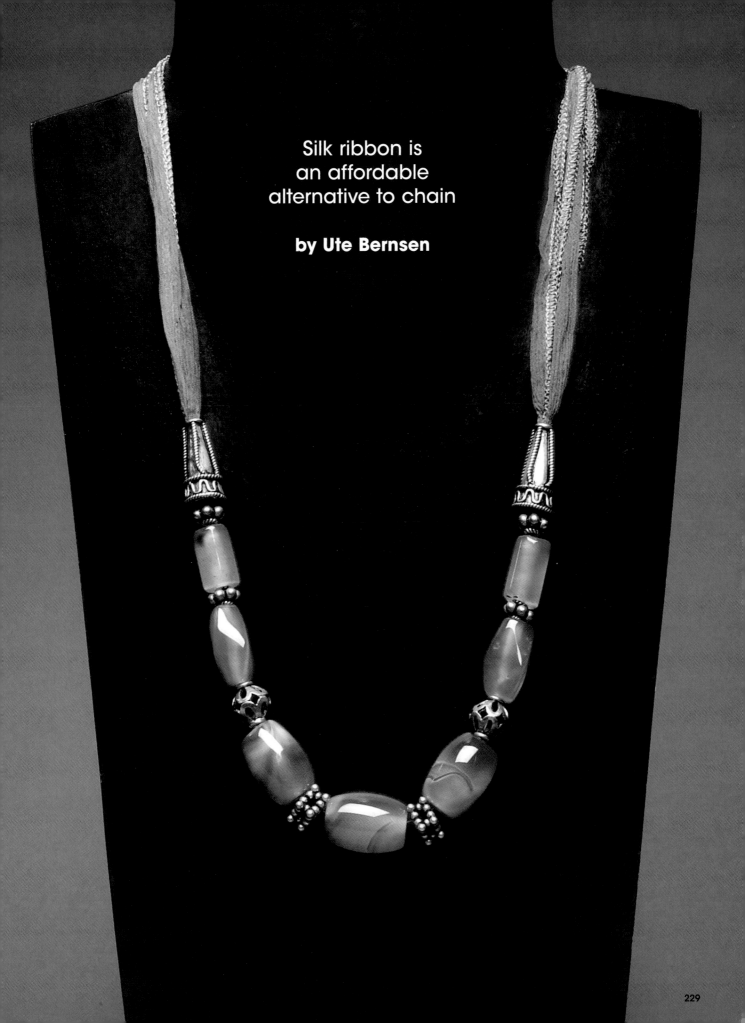

Silk ribbon is
an affordable
alternative to chain

by Ute Bernsen

1 earrings • On a head pin, string a spacer, a bead, and a cone. Make a plain loop (Basics).

2 Open the loop of an earring wire (Basics). Attach the dangle and close the loop. Make a second earring.

Design alternative

In a choker-length version, I used thinner silk cord and wove and knotted two colors around the beads.

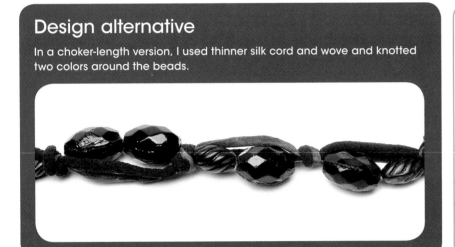

Supplies

necklace 26 in. (66 cm)
- **6–12** 12–18 mm oval or barrel-shaped beads
- **6–8** 8–11 mm silver beads
- **2** 5–10 mm flat spacers
- flexible beading wire, .014 or .015
- **2** 42 in. (1.1 m) 2 cm silk ribbons
- **6** in. (15 cm) 20-gauge half-hard wire
- **2** cones
- **2** crimp beads
- chainnose and roundnose pliers
- diagonal wire cutters
- crimping pliers (optional)

earrings
- **2** 12–18 mm oval or barrel-shaped beads
- **2** 1 mm spacers
- **2** 2-in. (5 cm) head pins
- **2** cones
- pair of earring wires
- chainnose and roundnose pliers
- diagonal wire cutters

Stir up some sweet delights

Hard candies such as Life Savers make great molds.

Create resin confections for a colorful bracelet

by Steven James

Have a little patience when you try this project — two-part resin requires precise measuring, mixing, and curing. Your first pieces might have bubbles in them (see Troubleshooting, p. 233). But don't worry: With practice, you'll get better. And once you see your favorite candy molded in resin, you'll love this new way to get your sugar fix.

1 resin candies • Cover your work surface with waxed paper. Mix equal parts of the part A and B mold elements. Work quickly; the putty will begin to harden after three minutes. Roll the putty into a ball and flatten it slightly. Place the putty on the waxed paper and press a candy in evenly. Wait 25 minutes and remove the candy.

2 Measure equal parts resin and hardener. Pour them into a plastic cup. Using a craft stick, stir slowly and gently for two minutes, scraping down the sides of the cup. Pour the mixture into a clean cup and stir with a clean craft stick for one minute.

❝As an art major in college, I produced large sculpture pieces using plastics and found objects. Resin gives me a chance to create sculptural pieces but work on a smaller, more intimate scale.**❞** –SJ

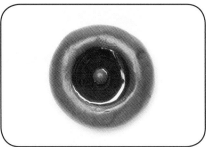

3 Add colorants as desired and stir gently.

4 Slowly pour the resin into the mold. Do not overfill. Allow to cure as directed, 24 to 72 hours. Cover the mold with a box so that dust doesn't fall into the resin.

5 Release the piece by gently flexing the mold. File the edges if necessary.

1 candy bracelet • Put on a dust mask. Place a resin candy on a wooden block. Drill a hole about ⅛ in. (3 mm) from the outer edge. Drill a second hole on the opposite side. Repeat to make five or six drilled candies.

2 Cut a 3-in. (7.6 cm) piece of wire. String one hole of a candy and make a set of wraps above it (Basics, p. 12). Make a wrapped loop (Basics) perpendicular to the candy. Repeat on the other side. Repeat for each candy.

3 Open a jump ring (Basics). Attach one loop of a candy to a loop of another candy. Close the jump ring. Repeat until you've connected all of the candies.

4 On one end, use a jump ring to attach a lobster claw clasp. Attach a jump ring on the other end.

Candy options

If you want to use gummy candies, like the ones at right, let them get stale before making the molds. Harder candies will yield better results. Also, candies with sugar stuck on the outside will have more of a textured, matte finish when cured.

Supplies

resin candies
- Castin' Craft EasyCast clear casting epoxy
- Castin' Craft EasyMold silicone putty
- Castin' Craft Transparent Resin Dye or Opaque Pigment in assorted colors
- hard candies such as Life Savers
- cardboard box (to cover pieces while they cure)
- disposable plastic cups
- emery board or sandpaper
- plastic gloves
- safety goggles
- waxed paper
- wooden craft sticks

candy bracelet
- **5-6** resin candies
- 30–36 in. (76–91 cm) 22- or 24-gauge half-hard wire
- **6-7** 5–6 mm jump rings
- lobster claw clasp
- chainnose and roundnose pliers
- diagonal wire cutters
- drill
- dust mask
- wooden block (for under the drill)

All about resin

Making molds

- Choose the least flawed pieces of candy to use in your molds. Any chips or bulges in the candy will transfer into the mold.
- Use clean, dry molds. Water residue can make your pieces cloudy.
- You can also place your molds on a Silpat baking mat instead of waxed paper.
- If you're making multiples of the same piece, make several molds. Otherwise, you'll need to wait while each piece cures before pouring another.

Warming up (to) resin

- Make sure your resin and hardener are at 70 to 80 degrees Fahrenheit when you mix them. Cold resin will dry cloudy or bubbly.
- Warm the bottles by placing them in cups of warm (not hot) water for a few minutes. Never microwave the bottles.
- To get rid of bubbles, use a propane torch or exhale over them with a straw. (It's the carbon dioxide, not the heat, that gets rid of the bubbles.)
- Cure at 70 to 85 degrees.
- You may be tempted to touch the resin while it's curing. Don't — your fingerprints will leave marks.

Troubleshooting

- If your finished pieces have soft spots, they can't be salvaged. Soft, tacky areas are the result of improper measuring or mixing of the resin.
- Bubbles can be the result of mistakes in different stages of the project. Make sure to measure precisely, stir slowly (don't whip), and pour carefully. Finally, cure the piece at a warm temperature. This bubbly Life Saver (enlarged to show detail) was my first piece. It looks nothing like its real-life counterpart (above).

Color notes

- Use transparent liquid colorants for a clear, glasslike look. The more you add, however, the darker and more opaque the color will appear.
- To make pastels, add white.
- Blend a color with white and a bit of black for a marbled effect.

Resin safety tips

- Wear gloves and safety goggles, and work in a well-ventilated area.
- Wear a dust mask when drilling cured resin pieces.
- Familiarize yourself with these instructions as well as the manufacturer's instructions before starting the project.

Take heart
make art

Pour your heartfelt sentiments into a playful pendant

by Jane Konkel

Artwork that contains text intrigues me. Whether the work is serious or whimsical, interpreting the embedded message is fascinating. Here, I trimmed a fortune from a fortune cookie then placed it in this heart pendant. The bezels are 4 mm deep, so you can overlap images, trinkets, and a special message in layers of resin.

1 To make the pendant, use a super giant punch to punch out a heart shape. Or, trace the pendant and cut out the image inside the lines.

2 Cover the inside surface of a heart pendant with a thin layer of craft glue. Lay the image inside the pendant. Use a cotton swab to press out bubbles. Allow the glue to dry.

3 Apply a thin layer of resin. Remove bubbles by popping them with a pin or toothpick, or by pushing them to the edge of the pendant. Allow to cure under a UV lamp.

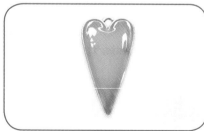

4 Glue additional images, text, or small charms to your pendant. Allow to dry. Fill the pendant with resin. Allow to cure under a UV lamp.

5 On a decorative head pin, string a bead. Make a wrapped loop (Basics, p. 12). Make eight to 10 bead units.

6 Cut an 18–24-in. (41–46 cm) piece of chain. Open a 7 mm jump ring (Basics) and attach the center link of chain, the pendant, and the bead units. Close the jump ring.

Paper punches come in handy, especially if you're making multiple pendants.

Time heals all wounds

66Look to old greeting cards, packaging, tea bags, and junk mail for your message99 –JK

Tips

• To prevent your text from bleeding, seal it in packing tape before you pour the resin.
• The UV lamp I used for this project is a 9-watt gel-curing professional nail dryer.
• Look for paint samples at your local hardware store to use as backgrounds for your pendants.

Supplies

necklace 24 in. (61 cm)
◆ 57 mm heart collage pendant
◆ decorative paper
◆ 2–4 mm text such as a fortune from a fortune cookie
◆ **1–3** 5–15 mm flat-back charms
◆ **8–10** 3–6 mm beads and crystals
◆ 18–24 in. (46–61 cm) chain, 8 mm links
◆ **8–10** 1½-in. (3.8 cm) decorative head pins
◆ 7 mm jump rings
◆ **2** 5 mm jump rings
◆ toggle clasp
◆ chainnose and roundnose pliers
◆ diagonal wire cutters
◆ cotton swab
◆ white craft glue
◆ pin or toothpick
◆ resin, such as Magic-Glos dimensional gloss
◆ scissors
◆ super giant punch by McGill Inc. (mcgillinc.com)
◆ UV lamp

7 On each end, use a 5 mm jump ring to attach half of a toggle clasp.

Photo-charm bracelet

Set tiny photographs in shapely bezels for an easy memory bracelet

by Irina Miech

Each time I wear my charm bracelet, I'm reminded of the seaside vacation I took with my boys. These crafty little charms make it really easy to encase a few favorite photos. Or, punch out some letters for a novel name bracelet.

Seaside memories
are crystal clear.

1 To make each picture frame charm, use a template to trace the desired shape onto a photo or decorative paper. Cut out the image.

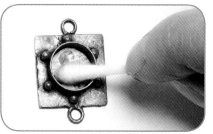

2 Cover the inside surface of each picture frame charm with a thin layer of Gem-Tac, G-S Hypo Cement, or craft glue. Lay the image down and press out air bubbles with a cotton swab. Allow the glue to dry.

3 Fill the charm with resin, such as Diamond Glaze. Remove air bubbles by popping them with a pin or pushing them to the edge of the charm. Allow to dry.

4 On a head pin, string a bicone crystal and make a wrapped loop (Basics, p. 12). Make four or five 6 mm bicone units and four or five 4 mm units.

5 Cut a 7–8-in. (18–20 cm) piece of chain. Open a jump ring (Basics) and attach a charm and the center link. Close the jump ring. On each side, attach the remaining charms about 1½ in. (3.8 cm) apart.

6 Use jump rings to attach picture frame charms between the charms.

7 Use jump rings to attach the crystal units. On each end, use a jump ring to attach half of a toggle clasp.

Tips

• Magic-Glos dimensional gloss requires UV light to cure. It dries in the sun (outdoors) or under a 6-watt or higher UV lamp.
• To prevent the image from bleeding, apply glue or decoupage as a sealant before adding resin.
• You can buy punches that make round, square, or oval shapes. Or, consider a set of alphabet punches (available from Jo-Ann Fabric and Craft Stores, joann.com).

Supplies

- ◆ **4–5** 20–30 mm picture frame charms
- ◆ **4–5** photos or decorative papers
- ◆ **4–5** 15–20 mm charms
- ◆ **4–5** 6 mm bicone crystals
- ◆ **4–5** 4 mm bicone crystals
- ◆ 7–8 in. (18–20 cm) chain, 5 mm links
- ◆ **8–10** 1½-in. (3.8 cm) head pins
- ◆ **18–22** 5 mm jump rings
- ◆ toggle clasp
- ◆ chainnose and roundnose pliers
- ◆ diagonal wire cutters
- ◆ cotton swab
- ◆ Diamond Glaze dimensional adhesive, or Magic-Glos dimensional gloss and UV light
- ◆ Gem-Tac, G-S Hypo Cement, or white craft glue
- ◆ pin or toothpick
- ◆ scissors
- ◆ template

"We loved Cape Cod. The scenery was beautiful no matter which way I turned." –IM

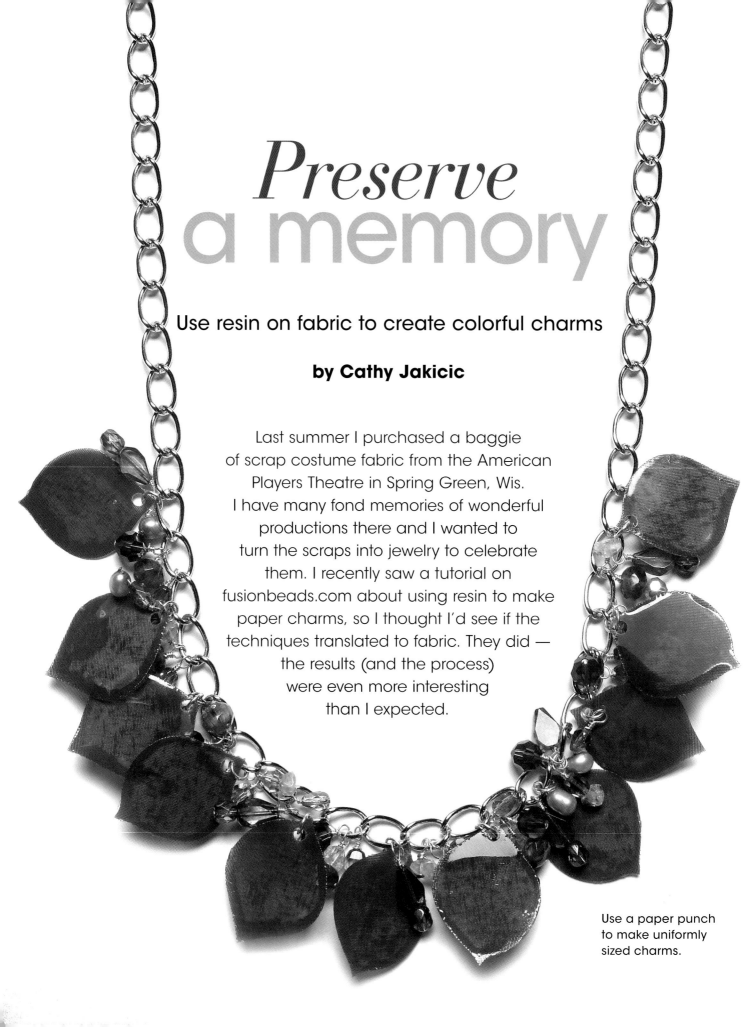

Preserve *a memory*

Use resin on fabric to create colorful charms

by Cathy Jakicic

Last summer I purchased a baggie of scrap costume fabric from the American Players Theatre in Spring Green, Wis. I have many fond memories of wonderful productions there and I wanted to turn the scraps into jewelry to celebrate them. I recently saw a tutorial on fusionbeads.com about using resin to make paper charms, so I thought I'd see if the techniques translated to fabric. They did — the results (and the process) were even more interesting than I expected.

Use a paper punch to make uniformly sized charms.

1 **fabric charms** • Apply craft glue to one side of the fabric and place the fabric on waxed paper or plastic wrap. Let dry. Repeat on the other side. The glue makes the fabric stiff enough for the paper punch.

2 Punch out a half-dozen more charms than you need for the necklace. It will save time later if you have some spares.

3 Place the charms on waxed paper or plastic wrap. Mix Ice Resin according to the package directions. With a sponge applicator, apply resin to one side of each charm. Let the charms dry. Repeat on the other side.

4 Use a hole punch to carefully punch a hole about 1/8 in. (3 mm) from the edge of each charm.

1 **necklace** • Cut an 18–20-in. (46–51 cm) piece of chain. Open a 5 mm jump ring (Basics, p. 12) and attach a charm and the center link. Close the jump ring. On each side, use jump rings to attach five charms, skipping a link between each.

2 On a head pin, string one or two beads. Make the first half of a wrapped loop (Basics). Make 52 bead units.

3 For each link with a charm, attach one bead unit to the link and another bead unit to the charm's jump ring. For each link between charms, attach three bead units. Complete the wraps as you go.

4 On each end, use a 7 mm jump ring to attach half of a clasp.

66 The more I experiment with resin, the more addicted I become.**99** –CJ

1 earrings • Using a charm left over from the necklace, punch a second hole on the opposite end. Following necklace step 2, make a bead unit. Attach the bead unit to one hole on the charm and complete the wraps.

2 Open a 5 mm jump ring (Basics) and attach the dangle and the loop of an earring wire. Close the jump ring. Make a second earring.

Supplies

fabric charms
- fabric scraps
- hole punch, 1/8 or 1/16 in.
- Ice Resin
- paper punch
- sponge paintbrush
- sponge eye shadow applicators
- waxed paper or plastic wrap
- white craft glue

necklace 18 in. (46 cm)
- **10–12** fabric charms
- **75–85** 6–14 mm beads and pearls, in a variety of shapes and colors
- 18–20 in. (46–51 cm) heavy cable chain, 10 mm links

- **52** 2-in. (5 cm) head pins
- **2** 7 mm jump rings
- **11** 5 mm jump rings
- toggle clasp
- chainnose and roundnose pliers
- diagonal wire cutters

earrings
- **2** fabric charms
- **2–4** 6–14 mm beads
- **2** 2-in. (5 cm) head pins
- **2** 5 mm jump rings
- pair of earring wires
- chainnose and roundnose pliers
- diagonal wire cutters
- hole punch, 1/8 or 1/16 in.

Tips

- Even though I sealed the fabric with craft glue, the resin still changed the color. The lavender color deepened and bits of green thread color emerged. Choose your beads after you see the final color of your charms.
- I used the 1/8-in. hole punch because I liked the look. A 1/16-in. punch will accommodate most jump rings.
- Lightweight, smooth fabric works best with the punches. If you can't resist using heavier fabric, use the punch to make a traceable paper template and cut the fabric shapes with scissors.
- Plan the number, type, and arrangement of bead units before starting necklace step 6. Decide whether you want a repeating pattern, random bunches of color, or some of both (I used some of both).

Coiled earrings

Set off a tower of accent beads with a simple wire spiral

by Felicia Cantillo

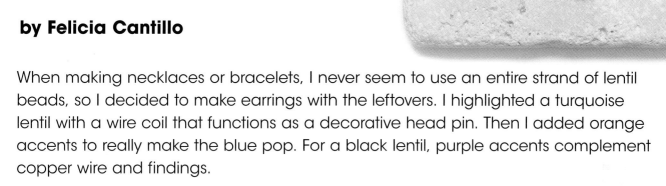

When making necklaces or bracelets, I never seem to use an entire strand of lentil beads, so I decided to make earrings with the leftovers. I highlighted a turquoise lentil with a wire coil that functions as a decorative head pin. Then I added orange accents to really make the blue pop. For a black lentil, purple accents complement copper wire and findings.

1 Cut a 1½-in. (3.8 cm) piece of 26-gauge wire. On one end, use the tip of your roundnose pliers to make a tiny loop. String an accent bead and make a wrapped loop (Basics, p. 12). Make 16 bead units.

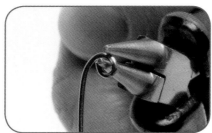

2 Cut a 5-in. (13 cm) piece of 20-gauge wire. On one end, use the tip of your roundnose pliers to make a tiny loop as in step 1.

3 Grasp the loop with chainnose pliers and continue coiling the wire with your fingers. Make the coil about ⁵⁄₁₆ in. (8 mm) in diameter.

4 String a lentil bead and bend the coil to the front of it. String: spacer, bead units, spacer, rondelle, cone. Make a plain loop (Basics).

5 Open the loop of an earring wire (Basics) and attach the dangle. Close the loop. Make a second earring.

Supplies

- **2** 20–22 mm lentil beads
- **2** 7–8 mm faceted rondelles
- **32** 4–5 mm accent beads in two or three colors
- **4** 3–4 mm flat spacers
- 10 in. (25 cm) 20-gauge wire
- 4 ft. (1.2 m) 26-gauge wire
- **2** 7–9 mm cones
- pair of earring wires
- chainnose and roundnose pliers
- diagonal wire cutters

Large-link chain works best for this bracelet.

Gather a
bead bouquet

Go on a treasure hunt for the makings of a floral stretch bracelet ◆ by Elizabeth O'Hara

To make this bracelet, I combined something old (wired glass beads) with something new (clearance sale jewelry) and added vintage flowers and leaves I received from a family estate division. Though you probably won't find the exact components I used, have fun searching thrift stores, sale tables, and bead shops for your own bounty of beads.

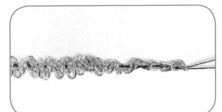

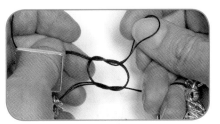

1 On a decorative head pin, string a large flower bead. Make a wrapped loop (Basics, p. 12). On a head pin, string a round bead. Make a plain loop (Basics). Make five large-flower units, eight to 12 small-flower/leaf units, and five round-bead units.

2 Cut an 18-in. (46 cm) piece of elastic cord and a 21–27-in. (53–69 cm) piece of chain. Fold the cord in half and string each link of the chain.

3 Tie a surgeon's knot (Basics) with the ends. Apply glue to the knot and trim the excess elastic.

4 Open a jump ring (Basics) and attach a large-flower unit, two or three small-flower or leaf units, and a link of chain. Close the jump ring. Repeat, attaching the clusters about 1½ in. (3.8 cm) apart.

5 Use jump rings to attach the round-bead units between the large-flower units.

Tip

The small wired glass flower and leaf beads on the left are old. You can find similar beads or make your own flower-bead units like the ones on the right with small flower beads and decorative head pins.

Supplies

- ◆ **5** 30 mm (large) flower beads, center drilled
- ◆ **5** 14 mm round beads
- ◆ **8–12** 10–20 mm (small) wired flowers and leaves, or **8–12** 10–20 mm flower beads and 1½-in. (3.8 cm) decorative head pins
- ◆ 21–27 in. (53–69 cm) chain, 8–12 mm links
- ◆ elastic cord
- ◆ **5** 1½-in. (3.8 cm) decorative head pins
- ◆ **5** 1½-in. (3.8 cm) head pins
- ◆ **18–22** 6–7 mm jump rings
- ◆ chainnose and roundnose pliers
- ◆ diagonal wire cutters
- ◆ G-S Hypo Cement

Jewels on parade

Colorful beads highlight a Texas tradition

by Heather Powers

Every year, San Antonio hosts Fiesta, a 10-day celebration with more than 100 events. Its most notable happening? The Battle of the Flowers parade, which began in 1891 as a way to honor the heroes of the Alamo. A mix of Texas pride and Mexican culture, this celebration boasts a rainbow of colors: *cascarones* (confetti-filled eggs that are cracked on your head), paper-flower crowns, and costumes worn by the crowd. I designed this necklace and earrings to echo the exuberance of the parade.

earrings • Make the earring components (p. 246). For each earring: Open a 7 mm jump ring (Basics, p. 12). Attach a glass teardrop bead and the loop of a single-rondelle connector. Close the jump ring.

2 Attach the other loop of the single-rondelle connector to the bottom loop of a triple-rondelle connector. Attach the loop of an earring wire.

Turn to p. 246 to make the necklace and earring components.

244

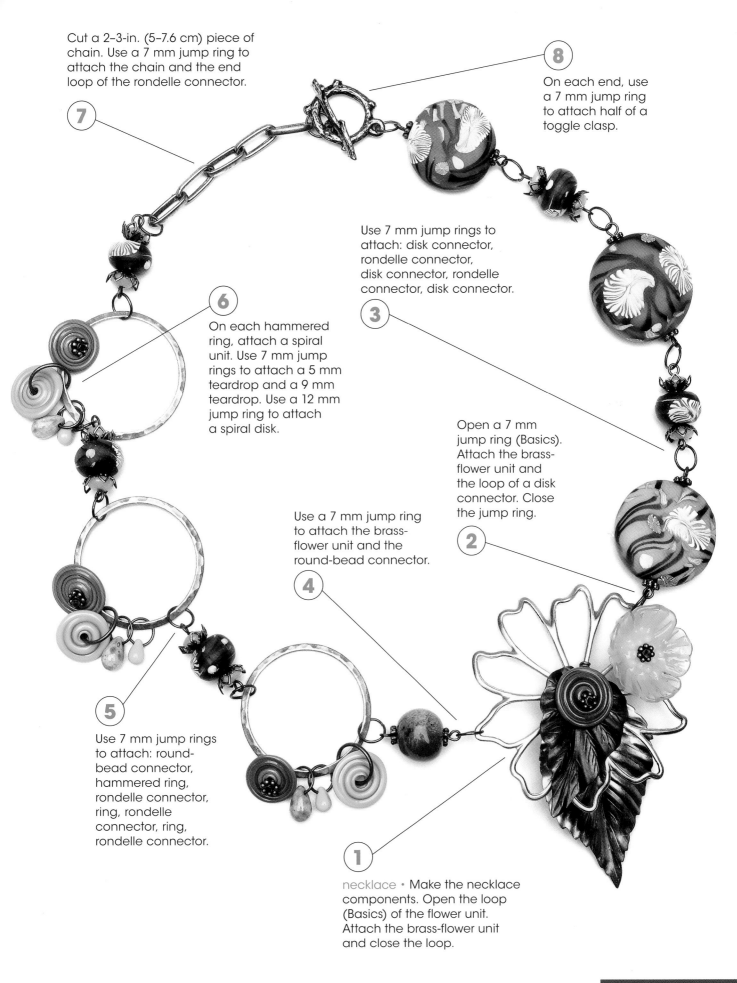

7
Cut a 2–3-in. (5–7.6 cm) piece of chain. Use a 7 mm jump ring to attach the chain and the end loop of the rondelle connector.

8
On each end, use a 7 mm jump ring to attach half of a toggle clasp.

3
Use 7 mm jump rings to attach: disk connector, rondelle connector, disk connector, rondelle connector, disk connector.

6
On each hammered ring, attach a spiral unit. Use 7 mm jump rings to attach a 5 mm teardrop and a 9 mm teardrop. Use a 12 mm jump ring to attach a spiral disk.

2
Open a 7 mm jump ring (Basics). Attach the brass-flower unit and the loop of a disk connector. Close the jump ring.

4
Use a 7 mm jump ring to attach the brass-flower unit and the round-bead connector.

5
Use 7 mm jump rings to attach: round-bead connector, hammered ring, rondelle connector, ring, rondelle connector, ring, rondelle connector.

1
necklace • Make the necklace components. Open the loop (Basics) of the flower unit. Attach the brass-flower unit and close the loop.

Necklace components

brass-flower unit • On a 1½-in. (3.8 cm) head pin, string: flat spacer, spiral disk bead, 38 mm leaf, center of a brass flower, 53 mm leaf. Wrap the wire around the flower to attach the components. Trim the excess wire.

spiral unit and flower unit • On a 1-in. (2.5 cm) head pin, string a flat spacer and a spiral disk bead. Make a plain loop (Basics). Make four spiral units (in one color) and one lampworked-flower unit.

disk connector • On a 1½-in. (3.8 cm) eye pin, string a flat spacer, a 23–28 mm polymer clay disk bead, and a flat spacer. Make a plain loop perpendicular to the first. Make three disk connectors.

rondelle connector • On a 1½-in. (3.8 cm) eye pin, string: 6 mm rondelle, bead cap, 12 mm polymer clay rondelle, bead cap, 6 mm rondelle. Make a plain loop perpendicular to the first. Make five rondelle connectors.

round-bead connector • On a 1½-in. (3.8 cm) eye pin, string a flat spacer, a 14 mm round bead, and a flat spacer. Make a plain loop perpendicular to the first. Make one round-bead connector.

Earring components

single-rondelle connector • On a 1½-in. (3.8 cm) eye pin, string a flat spacer, a 12 mm polymer clay rondelle, and a flat spacer. Make a plain loop (Basics) perpendicular to the first. Make two single-rondelle connectors.

triple-rondelle connector • On a 1½-in. (3.8 cm) eye pin, string: 6 mm rondelle, bead cap, 6 mm rondelle, bead cap, 6 mm rondelle, bead cap. Make a plain loop perpendicular to the first. Make two triple-rondelle connectors.

Tip
Artistic Wire in "gunmetal" matches the antiqued brass finish on these components. You can also use Parawire in Vintaj Bronze.

Supplies

necklace 20 in. (51 cm)

- 55 mm brass flower
- 53 mm brass beech leaf pendant
- 38 mm brass leaf pendant
- **3** 23–28 mm polymer clay disk beads
- 19–25 mm lampworked flower bead
- 14 mm round ceramic bead
- **7** 12–15 mm lampworked spiral disk beads, in two colors
- **5** 12 mm polymer clay rondelles
- **3** 9 mm glass teardrop beads
- **3** 5 mm glass teardrop beads
- **10** 6 mm rondelles
- **13** 4–5 mm flat spacers
- **10** 8 mm bead caps
- **3** 33 mm hammered rings
- 2–3 in. (5–7.6 cm) chain, 12 mm links

- **9** 1½-in. (3.8 cm) eye pins
- 1½-in. (3.8 cm) head pin
- **4** 1-in. (2.5 cm) head pins
- **3** 12 mm jump rings
- **21** 7 mm jump rings
- toggle clasp
- chainnose and roundnose pliers
- diagonal wire cutters

earrings

- **2** 12 mm polymer clay rondelles
- **2** 9 mm glass teardrop beads
- **6** 6 mm rondelles
- **4** 4–5 mm flat spacers
- **6** 8 mm bead caps
- **4** 1½-in. (3.8 cm) eye pins
- **2** 7 mm jump rings
- pair of earring wires
- chainnose and roundnose pliers
- diagonal wire cutters

Street vendors in San Antonio sell paper-flower crowns, a colorful Fiesta accessory.

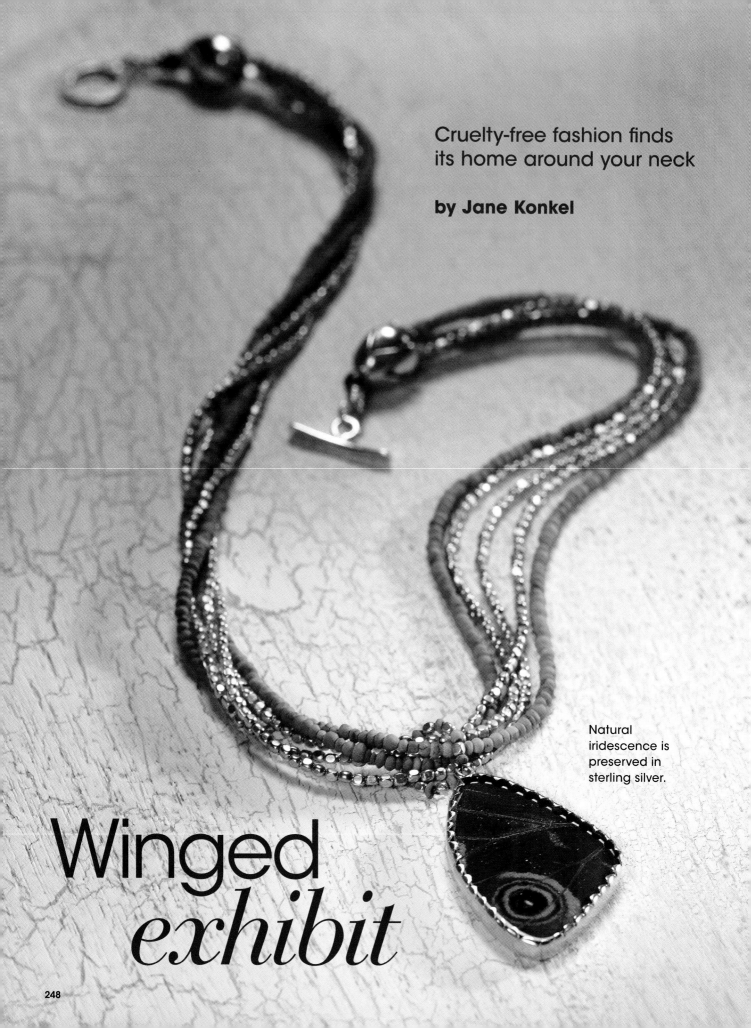

Cruelty-free fashion finds
its home around your neck

by Jane Konkel

Natural
iridescence is
preserved in
sterling silver.

Winged *exhibit*

The Peruvian Amazon is one of the most biologically diverse regions in the world and is home to more than 3,000 species of butterflies. When butterflies reach the end of their lives, they lay their eggs and die. They fall from the trees to the forest floor where licensed workers harvest the wings. The wings are encased in glass and sterling silver. The resulting pendants provide income for local families while preserving the rainforest's natural beauty.

Supplies

necklace 18 in. (46 cm)
- 40 mm shimmerwings pendant (Tika Imports, tikaimports.com)
- 2 16-in. (41 cm) strands 3 mm beads
- 3 24-in. (61 cm) strands 2 mm square spacers
- 2 4 mm spacers
- flexible beading wire, .010 or .012
- 6 in. (15 cm) 18-gauge wire
- 2 cones
- 11 crimp beads
- crimp cover
- toggle clasp
- chainnose and roundnose pliers
- diagonal wire cutters
- crimping pliers (optional)

earrings
- 10 3 mm beads
- 12 2 mm square spacers
- 48 in. (1.2 m) 24-gauge half-hard wire
- pair of earring wires
- chainnose pliers
- diagonal wire cutters
- Fiskars Right Angle mandrel (fiskarscrafts.com)

1 necklace • To make a bail: Cut a 3-in. (7.6 cm) piece of beading wire. Center a pendant. On each end, string ½ in. (1.3 cm) of alternating beads and spacers. On one end, string a crimp bead. String the other end through the crimp bead plus a few more beads. Crimp the crimp bead (Basics, p. 12). Close a crimp cover over the crimp.

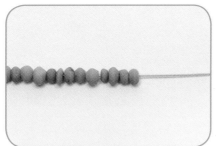

2 Cut five pieces of beading wire (Basics). On two wires, string beads until the strands are within 2 in. (5 cm) of the finished length. On three wires, string spacers until the strands are within 2 in. (5 cm) of the finished length.

3 Center the bail over all five strands.
Cut a 3-in. (7.6 cm) piece of 18-gauge wire. Make a wrapped loop on one end (Basics). Repeat.

4 On one side, on each wire, string a crimp bead and the loop. Repeat on the other side. Check the fit, and add or remove beads if necessary. Go back through the last few beads strung and tighten the wires. Crimp the crimp beads (Basics) and trim the excess wire. On each end, string a cone.

❝The wings in these pendants are collected at the end of the butterflies' natural life cycle and do not threaten their habitat.**❞** –JK

5 On each end, string a 4 mm spacer. Make the first half of a wrapped loop.

6 On each end, attach half of a clasp and complete the wraps.

Tips

• Stringing tiny beads one by one can be time consuming. Instead, thread your beading wire through the beads while they are still on their original strand.

• When finishing, we generally string a bead, a crimp bead, and a bead before the clasp. Because I wanted to hide the crimp beads inside the cones, I omitted the final bead after each crimp.

1 earrings • Cut a 24-in. (61 cm) piece of 24-gauge wire. Alternate six spacers and five beads on the wire. Center the beads.

2 Wrap each end three or four times around the largest part of a round mandrel, leaving a 2-in. (5 cm) tail on each end.

3 Wrap one tail five times around the wound wire. Wrap the other tail five times around the wire about ½ in. (1.3 cm) from the first set of wraps. Trim the excess wire.

4 Open the loop of an earring wire (Basics). Attach the hoop and close the loop. Make a second earring.

Design alternative

The shape of the earrings mimic the shape of a butterfly's wings. Because these beads have large holes, I strung them on 16-gauge wire and hammered it to create a matte finish and hold the beads in place.

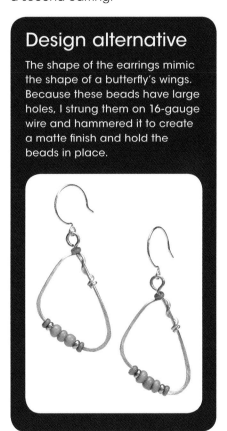

For a reversible reliquary, choose beads that highlight the spectacular colors of each side of the pendant.

Contributors

Theresa Drake Abelew can be found working in her studios on various painting, photography, writing, stained glass, or jewelry projects. Her company, 2 Dog Studios, is proud to donate a portion of all proceeds to animal rescue and adoption agencies. Contact Theresa at 2DogStudios@gmail.com or visit 2 Dog Studios on Facebook.

Lori Anderson is a full-time jewelry designer living in Easton, Md. When she designs at her kitchen table, she opts to watch CSI-type shows instead of listening to background music. Contact her at lori@lorianderson.net or visit lorianderson.net.

Contact **Carolina Angel** in care of Kalmbach Books.

Joan Bailey is a part-time jewelry artisan who sells her pieces at a local gallery and is expanding into metalsmithing. Contact her at jbailey@mwt.net.

As a world traveler, **Rupa Balachandar** likes to create jewelry that makes a statement. She regularly travels through Asia looking for components to make her jewelry and is pleased to share her finds through her website, rupab.com. Contact her via e-mail at info@rupab.com

Contact **Linda Aspenson Bergstrom** in care of Kalmbach Books.

An artist, silk painter, meditation teacher, and jewelry designer, **Ute Bernsen** is creating a course that combines these arts with meditation. Contact her at ute@silkpaintingisfun.com.

Paulette Biedenbender has been been beading since 1996 and currently teaches beading throughout the Milwaukee Metro area. Contact her via e-mail at h8winters@sbcglobal.net.

Heather Boardman is a glass artist and jewelry designer focusing her work on bright, fun colors and interesting shapes. Contact her via e-mail at heather@hmbstudios.com, or visit her website, hmbstudios.etsy.com.

Alaina Burnett blends her love for geology and archaeology in order to create a collection that is uniquely her own. She has been making jewelry since 1995 from her studio in Milwaukee, Wis. Contact her at alaina@alainaburnett.com or via her website, alainaburnett.com.

Christianne Camera co-owns Bella Bella! in Milwaukee, Wis. Contact her in care of Kalmbach Books.

Contact **Felicia Cantillo** in care of Kalmbach Books.

Contact **Mary Champion** in care of Kalmbach Books.

Contact **Laurie-Anne Clinton** in care of Kalmbach Books.

Candie Cooper is a trained metalsmith and accomplished author with a passion for combining unique materials and color combinations inspired by extensive travel and her years living in China. For a further look into her creative life, please visit candiecooper.com.

Dawn Davis is the owner of Simply Beadiful, LLC in Springfield, Mass. Contact her at simplybeadifulonline@yahoo.com or simplybeadiful.com.

Jess DiMeo and **Leah Hanoud** design, teach, and work at Turquoise-StringBeads in Fall River, Mass. Contact them at turq2000@turquoise-stringbeads.com.

Naomi Fujimoto is Senior Editor of *BeadStyle* magazine and the author of *Cool Jewels: Beading Projects for Teens*. Visit her blog at cooljewelsnaomi.blogspot.com, or contact her in care of *BeadStyle*.

Rebekah Gough is a jewelry artist who works from her home studio in Seattle, Wash. where she lives with her husband and two little boys. She can be contacted at rebekah.gough@gmail.com or via her website, orangepoppyjewelry.com.

Katie Hacker is an artist and author. She provides beading advice as the presenter of Beading Lessons on the public television series *Beads, Baubles & Jewels*, and she contributes how-to projects and articles to several magazines. Visit her website, katiehacker.com.

Monica Han Monica Han is an award-winning jewelry designer and teacher in Potomac, Md. She is also a CREATE YOUR STYLE with SWAROVSKI ELEMENTS Ambassador. Contact her via e-mail at mhan@dreambeads.biz.

Linda Arline Hartung is co-owner of Alacarte Clasps™ and WireLace®, and a CREATE YOUR STYLE with SWAROVSKI ELEMENTS Ambassador. Her designs and techniques have been featured in many beading and jewelry-making publications around the world. Contact her via e-mail at linda@alacarteclasps.com, or visit her websites, alacarteclasps.com or wirelace.com.

Catherine Hodge designs jewelry inspired by daydreams, textures, and color. Contact Catherine via her website, catherinemarissa.com.

Cathy Jakicic is Editor of *BeadStyle* magazine and the author of the book Hip Handmade Memory Jewelry. She has been creating jewelry for more than 15 years. Contact her via e-mail at cjakicic@beadstyle.com.

Armed with his mantra, "What are you gonna make today?," **Steven James** incorporates beads and jewelry making into home décor and everyday living. Visit his website, macaroniandglitter.com, or follow him at facebook.com/stevenjames.

Susan Kennedy makes glass and enamel beads in her home studio in Pittsburgh, Pa. To see more of her work, visit her website at suebeads.com or contact her at sue@suebeads.com.

Jane Konkel is Associate Editor of *BeadStyle*, and contributed several new designs to the book *Bead Journey*. Contact her via e-mail at jkonkel@beadstyle.com.

Sonia Kumar is a full-time student and self-taught jewelry designer from New Jersey. She can be contacted at sonia kumar92@yahoo or via her website, etsy.com/shop/catchalljewelry.

Contact Kelsey Lawler in care of Kalmbach Books.

Jewelry designer Monica Lueder enjoys adding an elegant flair to her designs. Contact her via e-mail at mdesign@wi.rr.com.

Carol McKinney approaches the creation of jewelry using her knowledge of interior design. "I start with a plan, choose a color palette, create a focal point, and design a piece that reflects the style and attitude of the person." Contact Carol McKinney at lemon.leopard@hotmail.com or through her website, lemonleopard.com.

Irina Miech is an artist, teacher, and the author of *Metal Clay for Beaders*, *More Metal Clay for Beaders*, *Inventive Metal Clay*, *Beautiful Wire Jewelry for Beaders*, and *Metal Clay Rings*. She also oversees her retail bead supply business and classroom studio, Eclectica and The Bead Studio in Brookfield, Wis., where she teaches classes in beading, wirework, and metal clay. Contact Irina at Eclectica, 262-641-0910, or via e-mail at eclecticainfo@sbcglobal.net.

Denise Yezbak Moore is a frequently published jewelry artist who dabbles in Art Clay Silver and elegant wire wrapping. She lives in Orange County, Calif., and can be contacted at yezy@aol.com or via her blog, deniseyezbakmoore.blogspot.com.

Polymer clay bead artist Heather Powers is the creative force behind Bead Cruise, Bead Week, and the Art Bead Scene. Visit her website, humblebeads.com, for more information or to contact her.

Elizabeth O'Hara spends her days ensconced in beads and has recently begun to design and create with seed beads, a new passion. Contact her at clubohara@charter.net or etsy.com/shop/Irishpoem.

Catherine Owsianiecki is a freelance writer and designer who resides in Bel Air, Md. Contact her via catherinefrances@ verizon.net or at mysite.verizon.net/ catherinefrances.

Antoinette D'Andria Rumely started collecting and beading nearly ten years ago. She feels fortunate, as she lives in New York City, which has tons of places to buy wonderful beads. Contact Antoinette at maxamarm@aol.com or through her website, CookieRumely.com.

Contact Toni Plastino in care of Kalmbach Books.

Tammy Powley is a jewelry designer and published author of various jewelry books, blogs, and a website. For more information, visit her website, tammy powley.com, or e-mail tammypowley@ yahoo.com.

Kate Purdy is a full-time jewelry artist who creates her unique designs in Coronado, Calif. Contact her at kate@ islandbangles.com or through her website, islandbangles.com.

Leah Rivers is a designer at Nina Designs and can be contacted at 1-800-336-NINA or ninadesigns.com.

Brenda Schweder is the author of the books *Steel Wire Jewelry*, *Junk to Jewelry*, and *Vintage Redux* and has contributed to *BeadStyle*, *Bead&Button*, and *Art Jewelry* magazines as well as many of Kalmbach's other special issues, compilations, and booklets. Contact her via e-mail at b@brendaschweder.com, or visit her website, brendaschweder.com.

Kim St. Jean is a full-time designer and instructor based from her bead store, Expressive Impressions in Charlotte, N.C. She can be reached at kim@kimstjean. com, or through her website, kimstjean.com.

Kellie Sutton recently opened her own bead store, Kellie's Bead Boutique, in Maple Ridge, British Columbia. Contact her via e-mail at kellie@kelliesbead boutique.com, or visit her website, kelliesbeadboutique.com.

Beads have been bossed around by Jessica Tiemens since 2002. They resisted for awhile, then succumbed to her brassy insistence. Now all the cake pans are occupied by her fantasies-in-progress. Contact Jessica via her websites, bright.circle@yahoo.com or paradoxmoxie.etsy.com.

Helene Tsigistras' jewelry has been featured in *BeadStyle* and *Bead&Button* magazines. She has also contributed designs to several books, including *Easy Birthstone Jewelry*. Contact her via e-mail at htsigistras@kalmbach.com.

Liisa Turunen is Head Designer and Instructor at Crystal Creations Bead Institute in West Palm Beach, Fla. She has been beading for 15 years. Contact Liisa at (561) 649-9909, via e-mail at info@ beadsgonewild.com, or visit her website, beadsgonewild.com.

Jenny Van is a microbiologist and jewelry designer based in Huntington Beach, Calif. Contact her via e-mail at jenny@beadsj. com, or visit her website, beadsj.com.

Stacy Werkheiser sews, beads, and crafts in her home state of Wisconsin and is an associate editor at *Bead&Button* magazine. Contact her in care of Kalmbach Books.

Ann Westby started making jewelry in 2001 and quickly discovered she had a passion for wirework. Contact Ann via her website, annwestby.com.

Contact Susan White in care of Kalmbach Books.

Jean Yates, of Westchester County, N.Y., enjoys creating beading tutorials and has written a jewelry design book titled *Links*. She is especially thankful to Artbeads.com for helping her family by supplying the beads used in her project. See her designs and contact her at prettykittydogmoonjewelry.com, or visit her blog at prettykittydogmoonjewelry. blogspot.com.

Index

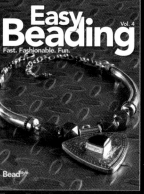

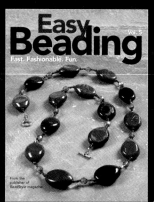